The American Spring

Amelia Stein

The American Spring

What we talk about when we talk about revolution

CONVERSATIONS WITH ARTISTS,
ACTIVISTS, AND THINKERS

KURT ANDERSEN, SAMPADA ARANKE, JULIA BACHA,
SEYLA BENHABIB, ARTHUR BLAUSTEIN, CRAIG CALHOUN,
PAUL CHAN, JEM COHEN, RY COODER, PETER DALE SCOTT,
DANA DART-MCLEAN, PETER DAVIS, CANDACE FALK,
LAWRENCE FERLINGHETTI, ROBERT FULLER, SAM GREEN,
JESSICA JACKSON HUTCHINS, COLTER JACOBSEN,
MARTIN JAY, KEVIN KILLIAN, LAWRENCE LESSIG, MICHAEL PARENTI,
FRANCES FOX PIVEN, LISA ROBERTSON, MARINA SITRIN,
MATTHEW STADLER, AND SOL YURICK

Skyhorse Publishing

To Margaret, Frank, and Terry

Skyhorse Publishing books may be purchased in bulk at special discounts for sales promotion, corporate gifts, fund-raising, or educational purposes. Special editions can also be created to specifications. For details, contact the Special Sales Department, Skyhorse Publishing, 307 West 36th Street, 11th Floor, New York, NY 10018 or info@skyhorsepublishing.com.

Skyhorse Publishing® is a registered trademark of Skyhorse Publishing, Inc.®, a Delaware corporation.

Visit our website at www.arcadepub.com.

10 9 8 7 6 5 4 3 2 1

Library of Congress Cataloging-in-Publication Data is available on file.

ISBN: 978-1-61608-747-0

Printed in Canada

Contents

INTRODUCTION

As the tide of Arab uprisings washed ashore in America and public parks and campuses around the country were occupied, people wanted to know: What does a revolution look like?

As the dual authorities of man and nature—Bloomberg's "army" and the arrival of winter—constricted the flow of the movement, people wanted to know: Is this it?

Since the eviction of protestors from encampments in many cities, smaller and more targeted occupations have continued. Workers in a Chicago factory occupied—with the support of their union—to protest layoffs. Teachers and students in Tucson staged a walkout to protest the removal of Chicano history books from the curriculum. Home foreclosures were disrupted, even avoided, by direct community action.

We have witnessed and participated in the unfolding of the past nine months—yet, we are no better attuned to the winds of change than we are able to determine if it was all just a momentary quickening.

A logical antidote to ambiguity is answers. History seems to suggest that ambiguities resolve, attended by an empirical explanation, as if answers exist that can not only clarify the future but resolve aspects of the present that are hard to label as "good" or even "promising."

Months ago, I contacted the artist Paul Chan. My email outlined a plan for a book that would secure definitive and helpful answers to a series of big questions about what was to become of Occupy Wall Street, of the increasingly aggressive discontentment with institutions of government and Congress, of *us*.

I received the following response:

"Hi A, These are important questions, and like most important questions, fairly unanswerable (definitively). And the people who have the answers are probably not much use (and dull besides). One thing: eternal questions are not really looking for answers, they are looking to be lived."

It took me some time to grasp Chan's meaning, but I believe it was simply this: The point is not to answer, but to ask.

The conversations in this book address what revolution and change can mean if we are open to new definitions. Occupy Wall Street demonstrates not only the need for a reinvigoration and repossession of both terms, but that this taking-back and enlivening is a process lived with others where the only appropriate discourse to support it ends with a question mark.

What does it mean to be political in the first place? Are we all political subjects from the outset or does it take a collective experience to radicalize the individual? Where do we position ourselves in relation to our current situation, to history and to the rest of the world? How do you document a moment of upheaval? How active is an idea? What does it mean to resist? What do we talk about when we talk about "revolution," if we talk about it at all?

These questions do not preclude the conceptual and ideal—but they do emphasize ideas and manifestations that are practical, social, and happening right now. Irresolution is immediate and dynamic. It is powerful because it is a different form from the watertight statements issued by governments and repeated in advocacy journalism, therefore not reducible to a sound bite. It is constructive because, in its articulation, it insists upon recognition of nuance and possibility. It is, as many in this book will emphasize, a radical alternative.

In *Bento's Sketchbook*, the author and critic John Berger smooths wrinkles between artistic, philosophical, and political impulses while allowing sufficient space for a motivating sense of outrage:

"To protest is to refuse being reduced to a zero and to an enforced silence. Therefore, at the very moment a protest is made, if it is made, there is a small victory . . . A protest is not principally a sacrifice made for some alternative, more just future; it is an inconsequential redemption of the present. . . ."

"How to live with the adjective *inconsequential*? The adjective is temporal. Perhaps a possible and adequate response is spatial? To go closer and closer to what is being redeemed from the present within the hearts of those who refuse the present's logic. A storyteller can sometimes do this."

To redeem the present while refusing its logic is the work of artists, activists, and thinkers. Irresolution is embedded in their practice. It is what compels them to engage and to be constructive, not necessarily with an end in mind. I believe that if anyone can speak to an understanding of revolution we have yet to really see, where the means *are* the ends, it is these people.

I should acknowledge that "storyteller" can bring to mind sentiment and a measure of abstraction. But this subversion of the term does not apply to the people interviewed here. Here, "storyteller" is simply a name for one who is creative in their approach to the present moment.

These were the people I wanted to hear from on the subject of "revolution," on the ways in which they question themselves and the structures of society and politics and on how they come to know change. Revolution is bound by narrative but these narratives are ultimately malleable. In fact, it is precisely non-prescriptive narratives that allow for struggles to arise and take shape. While it might appear that this book is full of answers, these are lived responses in the service of further questions, of an opening out rather than a locking down, and of—yes—a measure of hope.

I extend my gratitude to those who allowed me into their homes, offices, or otherwise for interviews. Thank you Miriam, Les, Celeste, and Edward. Thank you Tony and Jenn. Thank you Sinisa. Thank you patient and intuitive friends in New York, San Francisco, Melbourne, and Sydney who have put me in contact with many of the people in this book. Thank you to this particular time and place, which is precipitous but also, I believe, of consequence.

Amelia Stein
March 9, 2012
New York City

A NOTE ON
THE STRUCTURE

The intention of this book is to magnify and facilitate different aspects of a discussion already under way.

Revolution and social change are not dictated by isolated voices. They are elucidated and made manifest through dialogue grounded in experience and action. As such, these interviews are positioned in relation to one another rather than by theme.

Often, interviews that directly disagree or contravene are placed side by side. This is not an attempt to create a sense of contention. Rather, it is in the hope that the reader might carry information from one interview to the next and, on encountering perspectives that conflict, find each to hold equal potential for validity.

PAUL CHAN

The artist Paul Chan has exhibited internationally for over a decade at the Guggenheim Museum, the Serpentine Gallery (UK), and the 53rd Venice Biennale, among others. He became a publisher in 2010 when he founded Badlands Unlimited. Recent publications by Chan include *Wht is Lawlessness?* and *Wht is an Occupation?* as part of his *Wht is?* series of artist books.

Wht is Lawlessness? was first delivered as a talk at the New Museum in December 2011 as part of the "Propositions" series, in which Chan spoke about the intersection of knowledge, experience, art-making, and the laws—internal and external—that bind us.

Please explain to me what you wrote in our first correspondence.

My response to you was from your question about "what's next." I think we run into those questions a lot when we can't seem to find a way, concretely, to do something. And so in many ways, they are really philosophical questions. I don't want to suggest philosophical questions are not concrete questions, but they tend to be more abstract and they tend to be more reflective. And when those questions come up it seems not appropriate and maybe manifestly absurd to try to answer them because there's no real answer. The answer is in the doing, I suppose, of trying to live up to that question.

When I hear those questions, they seem to me to demand less an answer and more a way of living so that we embody those questions. A philosopher once said that the shape of a human being is a question mark. And I think he's more or less right. He was wrong about a lot of other things but he was more or less right in that regard. It feels right. And so

1

a question like what you asked, "What's next?" is a good question and to answer, in a way, we have to live as if we were going to be the next thing. I think we feel that, especially in Manhattan where everyone is trying to do the next thing. And that's great; it gives the city its energy.

Is the difficulty of the "what's next" question to do with a reluctance to be predictive?

I would say to me it's less a matter of predictive and more a matter of pre-scriptive. In [*Wht is Lawlessness?*], I start with the idea of a Daoist saying: that which can be taught is not worth learning. And I think the reason I used it is because we're surrounded by people who want to tell us what to do, how to do it, who to do it with, etcetera, and it's important that we're around people who are willing to share this information and knowledge with us, but my point was, if everyone's going to tell you what to do, how do you know who to listen to?

In a way, what I am saying to you now is: I don't want to be another one of those people who will tell you what to do—but that doesn't mean [one] stays silent. It perhaps takes another way of illuminating what it means to do things, by not telling people what to do but by sharing with someone what I've done, and by showing it as honestly and as complicat-edly as possible. Which is why, in the text, I tied the notion of knowledge to experience. This is a long philosophical tradition—the Daoists were not the only ones who thought of this. A lot of people know that they learn by doing, and by doing they come to know something. Experience is what was rightly called knowledge, in a way, as opposed to someone telling you, where you can't live it. Despite all the centuries of technol-ogy, despite all the philosophy, one of the only ways we can account for whether knowledge is real is whether we've lived it. And that's really it. If someone can espouse something that they themselves can't live with, we tend to think of them as a hypocrite. You're telling someone to do something that you yourself can't or won't do. And being a hypocrite is the surest way to be discredited, for us to know that the words are mere rhetoric. That hasn't changed.

Is there a way to be representative without being didactic?

That's a really good question, because I am sure there are many people who will tell you yes. I am not sure I want to be one of them. And the rea-son I don't want to do that is because of, I suppose, who I am and where I learn these things from, which is in art. I think in art, in my kind of art making, what I learn is what I get from the experience of making the thing. That somehow remakes me. I don't have anything in particular to say to you, but I have time on my hands to make things and in making it, ideally, hopefully, it changes me somehow. And the result of that process becomes something that someone else can experience. I think it's that type of experience that stops me from telling you. But again, you gotta tell people stuff. It's just human nature. Aristotle said that we're political animals. I think implicit within that idea is that, in politics, we have to communicate; we have to share; we have to congregate and collaborate; we have to live in a sociality. We can't live alone in a way that's like Theroux, or you become something like a Ted Kaczynski.

Is that what it means to you to be political?

I think it is a part of politics that we strangely forget a lot of the time. When we talk about politics, we tend to malign it for not doing enough. Whenever you mention U.S. Congress in relation to politics, for instance, it's always a kind of demeaning or derogatory term, as in "politics as usual," as in "nothing gets done." On the other hand, you see Occupy Wall Street and you imagine politics is something more liberating and more engaged, right? "We must engage in politics to change things." Within both of those things sociality is implicit, whether stopping change or moving forward with change. I think sociality becomes really important, sometimes more important than the change itself, because sociality is one part of the knowledge and experience equation that I talked about. No one practices politics on their own. We have to practice it with others. And the more there are of the others, the more possible the politics becomes. You need goals and events and actions to consolidate what that group identity is, but sociality is what makes that coalescence possible. If you only concentrate on the actions and events, without the sociality that allows the coalescence, nothing will come out. It will just be a disembodied direction. It's dialectical.

How would you describe your own position—as an activist, as an artist—within what you're describing?

I would start by saying that it's a good question and we would need something more concrete in order to go on talking about it. Because, in a way, what I feel about the questions is that they are good questions but that they are disembodied. Like with "what's next," you could say, "what's next for you," but that wouldn't embody the whole of what you're trying to get at, which I understand. You're trying to get at almost what they call a "spirit level," the Germans call it a *Zeitgeist*. That's implied in the question "what's next?" And to get at that you would have to speak at it on a level that I think is appropriate to that question. And that's, I think, why I am talking about "we." Because it's less about my sensibility, even though what I am talking about comes from the experience of what I know in politics and some things with art. It's just not at the same level in a way. What I am responding to is the enormity of [the question]. And the enormity of it demands, for me, speaking about it outside of my particular sensibility. It doesn't mean that what I say isn't informed by what I know. Obviously, it is. But it just doesn't seem right to me. I guess that's it.

Here's one way to get at it. Earlier in my work, in my career as an artist, the idea of utopia came up. So I did a lot of work and a lot of research trying to understand the idea of utopia. And what changed my mind completely was one line from one journalist, Seymour Hersh, a political journalist from the *New Yorker*, famous for breaking the story of the My Lai massacre. He wrote this piece about how the Bush Administration were utopians, which completely upended the idea of a utopia. We would believe that a utopia is something a little more beautiful than what we had in the years of the Bush Administration. He accused them of being utopians because they refused to see reality as it was. They refused a historical understanding of what they were enveloped in, regarding their foreign policy. All they wanted was to stick to what they imagined would be the bright future of the Middle East, and they were willing to do anything to make it happen. So he accused them of not "being here," in a way.

But isn't that divorcing utopia from any sense of values?

I don't know if it divorces it as much as it puts another spin on utopianism that does pan out, historically. If you and I think of examples of utopias, in my mind a full third or maybe half of them turned out really bad. Maybe more than half. Maybe 90 percent turned out really bad. A lot of things happen over the course of time: did the Khmer Rouge start out with the idea that they were going to murder a third of their country? Probably not. The French Revolution probably did not plan on the Thermidor, the Great Terror, but it happened. I'm from China and the Maoist revolution was one of the great successes of communism, but it turned into less than communism, let's just say. Even the experiment of America has changed somewhat. So the question to me is, how much stake we can place in the idea of utopianism as a kind of North Star of hope, given that maybe one of the founding characteristics of utopians is their inability to see here for what it is, while pursuing what they believe is to be the "bright future" as long as people believe specifically what they believe. In the history of the Western and Eastern world, there are plenty of examples of beautiful utopian philosophies in literature—I don't deny that. Political utopianism is much more complicated.

In a weird way, this is a circuitous way back to the question of "what's next?" As we're talking, I've realized I am talking around that question because I may be more interested in what's *here*, as opposed to what's next. My work as an artist and perhaps my work as a thinker is to give some semblance of representation to ways in which we can be more *here*. To me, it's not up to me to say what's next because I don't have that dimension in me. But I am most interested in trying to see what's here. I wrote it in my talk [*Wht is Lawlessness?*] in a line that said: "Art is more real than reality." And what that gets at is the spirit of what I am talking about: that it's hard to be *here*, you know what I mean? I think the feeling that we can be elsewhere while we're here causes a lot of complications, and these complications do not allow us to see the forest or the trees, but we need to see them both in order to see them both, I suppose. And art teaches you that. I need to pay attention, because I make things, about what's happening as I do it, so that I can learn from the process to see what else is happening. You can do that politically, but it takes a kind of sociality, a realization that you're talking to and dealing with human beings—as opposed to consumers or followers or apostles or people that you can use.

Is it awareness that you're talking about?

Definitely. I think that's a good way of putting it. It's being aware of so many things. Being sensitive—and when I say sensitive I mean using all the senses, to know where you are. And I mean that in as expanded a sense as possible; to know where one is, not only in a place but in a time and context. Also, maybe, within a tradition. Not to follow [a tradition], just to be aware. We live in a time we could almost call the "Age of Distraction." So much of our lives are lived in perpetual distraction, because so many things compel us to be distracted. And it's difficult to be aware when you're perpetually distracted. But that awareness allows us to make distinctions about what's important and what's not, which then give us courage and the possibility of making choices that we feel good about.

Or at least better about, so we don't feel like we are being pushed around, like we're just a feather in the wind. Paul Valery had a beautiful line that one should be like a bird, not like a feather. That's the feeling when one is aware. You're like a bird. When we're aware, we have choices I think. We feel like we're not as trapped.

In Wht is Lawlessness?, *there is a reference to internal forces and external forces. Where does choice fit into that?*

Law can be thought of at least in two ways: external law and internal law. External law is laws against littering, laws against hurting other people. It's an external system or authority that says, "You cannot do this." Inner law, on the other hand, is connected historically to the laws of nature: What is our tendency? Through our experiences and perhaps through our genetics we've developed a nature. We have certain tendencies that we seem to follow even though no one told us to. Choice, in a strange way, is related to the idea of reason in both cases. Philosophically, the idea of reason—an understanding of cause and effect—gives us a sense of will, helps us negotiate both, because if you don't have reason, you're blindly following either external law or inner law. With external law you're blindly following the law of the State without questioning what it's for or your place in it. On the other hand, if you don't have a sense of reason against inner law, you're essentially floating by the whims of your compulsions—those tendencies that are our own, but may not have our welfare in mind as they replicate themselves. I think, philosophically, it's the idea of reason, which sounds completely boring.

I've become convinced that this idea of reason is more useful and more important than ever. It's not reason like that guy you meet who gets in arguments and loves to be right. I mean reason like being able to see the causes and effects of things, which is part and parcel of being aware. Being aware that when you hit someone, they're probably going to get hurt and they're probably going to get mad. It's strange to talk about as an artist because we are the ciphers of freedom, you know? Our job, if we take it seriously, is that we make things that are emblems of freedom. But I think one of the reasons why I wrote [*Wht is Lawlessness?*] is to try to get at the idea that, as free as we may be, we're not completely free. We're still lawful people. We follow another law, and the question is: Do we have any say in breaking that law as well, and is there a freer freedom in breaking the law of our inner tendencies?

When you pose questions like that, is it to give yourself cause to think about them but not answer them definitively?

You know, I think I wasn't lying when I emailed you. I think the questions that are most interesting to me are the ones that there seems to be no satisfying answer to, and the reason there is no satisfying answer is because they're not to be answered. They're, in a way, to be lived and to be renewed. I had this funny dinner once with Tom Hayden, a famous '60s organizer and activist and part of the Students for a Democratic Society. He was railing against younger activists, and said if only they had listened to his generation, we wouldn't be in the mess we're in now. I think what he doesn't realize is that it can't work that way because each generation needs their own way of understanding who the enemy is, even if the enemy is the same. Who they were fighting in the '60s and '70s is not that different from who Occupy Wall Street is fighting now. It's still greed, corruption, injustice, and inequality, but we can't use their language because it's *their* language. Each generation has developed their own set of questions to combat perhaps even the same things, so that the fight can be theirs. And I think the sense of renewal of the questions is one way we inhabit the things that we care about so that we become more engaged.

Is experience creative?

It certainly can be. One hopes it is. And what would be creative experience as opposed to uncreative experience? Uncreative experience would be deadening.

I would put it to you that part of what is so constructive or real about Occupy Wall Street is that it is experience but it also facilitates awareness and so, for that reason, it's creative.

I would agree. I think what's different about Occupy Wall Street is precisely that one can experience it as it learns from itself. Everyone knows that to understand Occupy Wall Street you actually have to occupy with other people in Zuccotti Park. That was the feeling: You can explain it, but you should just go there and see it for yourself. I think that is symptomatic of what we're talking about. Within the example of Occupy Wall Street, that idea of knowledge being in a primary relationship with experience is real. You experience it, and you learn. It's the best kind of political engagement. Now that Zuccotti Park is no longer occupied, what we see is Phase 2 of Occupy Wall Street here in New York, where people are trying to figure out what to do next. And I can already sense that there is a kind of malaise that comes from being in the winter, from not having a concrete experience like occupying a physical space to fulfill. You can feel the idea of knowledge and experience being disentangled in a way, with more knowledge being developed, without having the requisite experience to fulfill it. So I think that's a real question, which is why OWS are continuing to think about a lot of other actions. They need more experiences, because that's how we come to know. It seems right to me.

I would say that the desire to push from unaware experience into aware experience would be new to a lot of people, especially young people.

I came from a generation in the U.S. where the protest movements were largely around anti-globalization and then, after that, the Iraq War—so from 2000 to 2003, with 9/11 in between. That was my generation. This generation of folks in their twenties—I mean, it's intergenerational but primarily I see the most energy coming from twenty- and early thirty-year-olds—may not have had that experience but they have their own sense of what's wrong, and a crumbling sense of economic opportunity. It's important that they see reality for what it is, and that's what it is. In a way, Occupy Wall Street and the young people who are part of it see reality more clearly than the politicians and the bankers who seem to run this country. They can't ignore the fact that they have $50,000 debt and they can't pay for it. They can't ignore the fact that banks got bailed out but homes were foreclosed, that public money was diverted to two wars that no one wanted. And the more they experience Occupy Wall Street, the more that intuitive knowledge they have about something not being right becomes manifest in reality, and has the potential to create a new knowledge by being with other people.

We see now in the U.S. a whole new generation of people realizing that they are the public, and that by being the public things can shift. But each generation has to find that, and the rest of us have to simply support it if we can't be a part of it. We just shouldn't be like a Tom Hayden, basically. Which is unfair, because he sent me an email a couple of days later, but I was pissed off. Each generation has to find its own way to combat and engage in these things, otherwise it wouldn't be theirs. To blame people for not following you is to say you should ditch your own authority for his. No one owns enemies; we have to make our enemies our own. How else would we engage in a way that makes it worthy of a fight?

LAWRENCE LESSIG

Lawrence Lessig is the director of the Edmond J. Safra Center for Ethics at Harvard University and the Roy L. Furman Professor of Law and Leadership at Harvard Law School. He is also a founding board member of Creative Commons and an advocate of "free culture."

It was a shock indeed to hear him say that contemporary America is "fucked," but an even greater shock to hear—and read, in his most recent books, *Republic, Lost: How Money Corrupts Congress—and a Plan to Stop It* and *One Way Forward: The Outsider's Guide to Fixing the Republic—* that he has a clear plan through which this situation might be altered.

In the preface of Republic, Lost, *you wrote that things were not necessarily bad enough for people to act. That was before Occupy Wall Street. What motivates people to take action?*

I think there are two things: one is to have framed the right kind of wrong. So, it's easy to motivate people to act when it seems like there's evil on the other side. The second thing is that there has to seem to be something that could come out of [action]; some hope, a reason, that something could change. In the preface of *Republic, Lost*, what I was saying was more that there weren't any clear bad actors here—there are a lot of people nobody likes much, but it's not like at the center of the system you have Rod Blagojevichs everywhere—and that was the opposite of a motivator; a dis-motivator or anti-motivator.

What is the process through which a society comes to identify with their capacity to enact change?

One of the core parts of democracy is that people have to see it work. They have to recognize that there's a hard decision that has to be made

9

and then they have to see people resolving it and that there's some kind of follow-through on the other side. I remember once I was in the Republic of Georgia when [Eduard] Shevardnadze was in charge, and the secretary of state said to me, "What was the most important day in American history?" I had no clue. He said, "March 4th, 1801." I didn't know what that was. He said, "That was the day when the American government peacefully transferred power from one political organization to another." It's that day that convinced the American public that democracy was possible, and it's that sort of day that Georgia has never had since before the war. Every change has been through violence of some form and it's the same kind of thing here. I think what's happened in the United States is that we saw in 2008 these huge aspirations for change, people expected there would be a lot of change, nothing happened and so people disengaged from the democratic process because they say, "What's the use? What's the reason? If we're going to get change we need to do it some other way, like occupying Wall Street."

So it's really the belief in possibility that's crucial?

Crucial, yeah.

In response to a question posed to you on Formspring, you wrote: "The solution is deemed impossible so people ignore the problem."

If you have in your head the sense that change isn't feasible or possible or allowed, then you learn to ignore the problem. There are lots of problems conceived of if you imagine the world is totally plastic, problems that we just don't notice—for example, that we die. That's a really big problem. If we could just make it so that nobody died from old age we'd be talking about the problem of death. But we don't even think about that as a problem because it's not feasible to talk about ending death. It might be some day, but that's not where we are now so we don't even see it as a problem. Sometimes I imagine, what if we could change the weather? The government would just type into a computer, "Rain over New York today." All of a sudden we'd have a problem: When should it rain over New York? What is the justice of rain? But that's not in the realm of feasibility so it's not identified as a problem. So, a problem inherently ties to a feasible solution and in that sense the very naming of something as a problem is optimistic, because it means that we can see how it could be changed, as opposed to the things that we couldn't conceive of changing.

In Republic, Lost, *you wrote that the way forward would be a path between academia and activism. Both are often accused of being out of touch with the rest of society. How can they come together in a relevant and useful way?*

Activists are in the business of taking ideas and turning them into action. Academics are in the business of taking observations and turning them into ideas, so there's an obvious chain there: We have observations, we produce ideas, we hand the ideas over to the activists, the activists turn them into action. And as I say in the book, I sometimes think that these fields are too disparate and they don't want to communicate. It's obviously necessary for them to work together so that one can feed the other—the activist can learn something from the academic, the academic can feel like it's worthwhile to figure out what the right answer is because they can see it translated into something useful. But each of these fields closes off to the other and that's ultimately destructive for both.

It might be that the categories of "activist" and "academic" are under-specified. A lot of academics don't want to feed activism because they think that undermines their neutrality, and some academics have no problem feeding activism because the academic subject or field itself speaks to an active end. Lawyers are about enabling justice in certain circumstances, so lawyers are less troubled by also being activists as opposed to . . . I don't know, economists. And the same with activists: Some activists surely have an anarchist streak to them but some don't.

What is common between academia and activism?

Both have a rationality to them, in the sense that they confront something; they understand how it could be different and then they believe they should be able to intervene to make it different. Both of them don't take structures as given and react as much about the structures as about any particular injustice within [the structures]. And that's obviously not an attitude everyone has. I remember once listening to a talk back radio show in 1988. A woman called in and said, "You know, I've been getting my telephone bills every month for the last thirty years and they've always been quite reasonable, $20 a month, but last month it was $27,000." So the activist or the academic would look at that and say there was obviously a problem with the way the billing worked and that they would go and fix it. But this woman was asking the host if the phone company would let her pay the bill in monthly installments. Her assumption was that this was reality and she'd just have to live with it, that she was going to have to pay off what she didn't incur. That response is incomprehensible to the activist or the academic. But there are many people, maybe the vast majority of people, for whom this is the standard response.

Why?

I think many people feel like things are dealt to them and they will just have to cope with them. They can suffer and they can be angry or upset but they just have to get on with it. How else do you explain people's relationship to their credit cards? There are people paying 25 percent interest. They just think about it as: "As long as I meet my monthly payment, I get all this money for free." They don't even put one and one together—literally, they don't add the costs. It's insane to pay 25 percent interest but they accept the craziness. They don't rationalize it; they don't understand it.

Is it a lack of rationality or something else?

It might just be a lack of capacity, in that they don't have time for it. There was a woman I knew, an entrepreneur, during one of the first tech crunch bubbles circa 2001. She described to me how she was working twenty-one hours a day, and she watched her stock portfolio go from being worth something like $100 million to $1 million. I said, "Why didn't you just sell it off?" She said, "I didn't have time." You didn't have time? It's $100 million. Just stay home one day and call your broker. But I think a lot of people are in that position. They're working three jobs, they've got their kids' tuition, it's all they can do to put food on the table, how are they going to deal with that situation? They're not. They're just going to get up each day and do what they have to do.

You have described the management of corruption as an aspect of modern life. Whose responsibility is this management?

The first line of responsibility is the institution of Congress itself. It should structure itself so that we can trust it. And, failing that, the second line of responsibility is we—the outsiders—who need to get together and do something to get Congress to move.

How do you imagine that would work?

In my framework, we look at politics as being about left and right but it's also about inside and outside. What we've seen in the last five or ten years is wave after wave of outsider politics; a sort of fury at something going on inside the government. [Grassroots movements] could mature, not in the sense that everybody gets together and sings "Kumbaya," but in the sense that people start to think strategically in different camps—so that the Occupiers recognize not that they share values with the Tea Party, but that both of them have a common enemy in the current corruption of the way government works. If they could recognize their common enemy, and organize to defeat it, then there's a potential that they could amass enough political power to force the system to change.

You argue that Occupy's potential lies in the unification of left and right.

We could just share enough to agree that we ought to be within a system of democracy that fairly adjudicates our differences. Votes ought to be counted; votes ought to determine. I don't have to agree with you about substantive values to agree that that's the structure in which we should be operating. Or say I don't agree with you about egalitarianism or gay rights—there are substantive issues that we generally disagree on in our society, but we should be able to bracket those in order to recognize that there's something about the constitutional structure that is deeply flawed and to be able to stand back from the substantive disagreements and talk about how we fix that flaw so that we can have confidence again in the system that might adjudicate our differences. I know historically it's been possible for people to have that point of reflection. I've spoken a bunch of times about the founding of the nation where people who believed in slavery sat down with people who thought slavery was the moral abomination of the age. They can bracket that disagreement enough to have an argument about what the structure of the Constitution should be and how we could save the nation from certain destruction. It's happened and we should be able to reconstruct it today, not to think about the whole structure of society, but just to think about one tiny corner where obvious corruption has been allowed to emerge where we should be able to redress and reverse it.

Why hasn't it happened yet?

I think a lot of it has to do with the business model of organizing. It's almost impossible not to polarize, because there's no return for moderation. You want to get your Tea Party rallied up, you call the Occupiers a bunch of America-hating anarchists. Then you've got the Occupiers rallied up about the racist Tea Party people. It's a way to build and sustain the immense passion necessary to push your substantive vision forward, and I get that. Nothing's more fun than reflecting on why we're good and they're bad. But if you think that we actually *need* them if we're going to get real constitutional change, then you have to find a way to talk that doesn't necessarily alienate [the other side].

Is it possible to distinguish between systems and institutions as corrupt, and the corruption of the people within them?

You know, I have no problem saying people are responsible. I have no problem saying members of Congress are responsible for the dismal state of Congress. Collectively, Congress ought to act in a way that eliminates the economy of influence that produces corruption. But it's a leap to go from that to: therefore, Congressman X is responsible for the corruption of Congress. Because he's not, he's only able to do something about it if he can act with the support of half or two thirds of the body. How do I understand if he can do that or not? I can say to him, "Well, you should be devoting 100 percent of your time to the task of eliminating this kind of corruption inside the system." And he could fairly say to me, "Well, if I did that, the chance of succeeding is 0.001 percent and so the return from that behavior is pretty low, but if I spend my time worrying about welfare for spouses of veterans then I could actually do something good for society." In that trade-off, it's hard for me to say, "You're an evil person," or even "You're a bad person." So it's not analytically simple, but it's enormously pedestrian in the sense that we understand this very well; we live this all the time in our lives. We are constantly within structures which in some sense are evil or do harm in the world. As an American, I recognize that we do all sorts of horrible things and, you know, I just want to say that there's a difference in the way that I am related to that evil and the way that George W. Bush or Barack Obama is related to that evil. And there's a difference in the way a congressman is related to the corruption of Congress and the way that Randy "Duke" Cunningham is related to the corruption of Congress. There's just that difference.

Would a constitutional convention be revolutionary action?

There are two kinds of constitutional conventions: one is a constitutional convention and the other is an Article 5 constitutional convention, and I have only talked about the latter. That, I don't think, would be revolutionary because it would be in the terms of the existing Constitution. The Constitution says that you can create this thing called a constitutional convention, which can propose amendments, which can then be ratified through the mechanisms specified in Article 5. But, reserved to us as people within a republic is the right, as Jefferson put it, to alter or abolish our government at any time. We, in principle, look at it as crazy that the Occupiers got together and talked about creating their own [government] but in principle that's the theory of American government: If enough of us get together and say, "To hell with this stupid system, we're going to withdraw our power and reconstitute in a different government," we can do that, and that would be revolutionary. So there are people who think we need that kind of revolution. Maybe we do. But I'm talking about intra-constitutional revolution.

What changes do you think are absolutely necessary?

The changes that have to come about are: A. a commitment to public funding, B. a commitment to giving Congress the power to limit independent expenditures. There are other changes you could have, but those are the only changes I think are necessary. The way that that's going to be brought about I think requires constitutional change. The only constitutional change we're ever going to see is if it's forced through the convention process, but I do believe that the convention process should be a convention process on the model of what Iceland has just done: Iceland created these citizen panels and a citizen drafting commission and a citizen process to produce a constitution that will decide by referendum. I think we could have a citizen-driven convention, which comes up with proposed amendments that then get sent out to the public.

What is your dream situation? Is that it?

My dream situation would be that tomorrow Congress would come to its senses and pass public funding and propose an amendment to change the Citizens United's decision and thirty-eight states would ratify it next week, so we can go back to our lives. There are people in politics who have politics and that's their life. I don't want to do that. I want to go back to my life of scholarship. I have a book on constitutional theory I've been writing for twelve years. I want to do that, I don't want to do this.

What is the responsibility you feel to contend with these issues?

I feel like . . . a couple of things. I think we're fucked, number one. I think the country is in a really terrible space, and that's not just bad for America, it's bad for the world. And I don't believe, number two, that the insiders will ever fix it. I care about it, not just because I have a romantic conception of the United States but because I have three children and I want them to have a place to be proud of and grow up in where they can be respectful of themselves, their rights, and the rights of those around them. I feel invested in it. I don't feel responsible in the sense that somebody might tell me I wasn't doing my duty if I just went back to my life, but I feel responsible for it in the sense that I feel it's not enough to just go on with life right now.

What relationship do you see between creativity and change?

They're deeply connected in the sense that a creative sort is playful and can imagine putting things together in different ways, and has the capacity to think through: What happens if I move this or add this? Like a jazz musician—what happens if I build on this?—they can envision it. I think that you need to be able to do that to change in a responsible way. You can flail about on the floor but if you want to bring about change you have to have some sense of a model of how doing one thing will affect something else. It's one of my frustrations with [the Occupy Wall Street] movement, I constantly feel like I confront people who are passionate for change but you get them to say how something is going to bring about anything and they have no thoughts about it. It's like how people out there are talking about a constitutional amendment which will say that corporations are not persons. What the hell would that do? OK, corporations are not persons. But still, a tiny slice of America funds political campaigns and it's not even clear that [an amendment to state that corporations are not persons] entails that Citizens United would be reversed. It doesn't change anything, yet people can't think through more than two steps down the road. But I think creative sorts play that game, it's in their head all the time.

Let's talk about the concentration of campaign funding in the 0.05 percent. To be able to undo this would, in a sense, democratize power and influence.

It's hard to do this analytically but it's important, I think, to distinguish between people who are pushing for egalitarianism in influence and people who are pushing for the end of corruption in influence. And although those overlap in certain ways, they're very distinct. I am opposed to the 0.05 percent controlling as much as they do because I see the way in which that corrupts a process where representatives are supposed to be dependent on the people alone. I don't oppose the 0.05 percent having the power that they do because I have some abstract conception of equality in my head. One way to test that is: Imagine a State said that unions have too much power because it's too easy for them to organize their members to turn out to vote, therefore we're going to ban unions from directing their members as to how to vote. That's very analogous to people's concern about corporate power. I think that type of regulation—limiting corporate power—is fundamentally illegitimate because organizing votes is the essence of what power in a democracy is supposed to be about. I agree it's unequal, I don't have as much power as a union leader does; a union leader says something and 400,000 people follow it. That's amazing power relative to me. But that kind of inequality is, I think, inherent in the nature of a system like democracy and I think it's improper to interfere.

I embrace the conception of Federalist 52 of a representative democracy dependent on the people, but I have no idea what that dependency might mean. All I know is what it doesn't mean: what it doesn't mean is a democracy where the representatives are also dependent on the funders when the funders are not the people, because therefore they're not dependent on the people alone. So I can tell you what doesn't satisfy that model, but I can't begin to tell you what does satisfy that model. How you structure a democracy within the model of dependent upon the people alone is really hard. A lot of people think that we have to have the constant ability to punish and recall representatives who don't behave the way we want them to. Jenny Mansbridge has a theory that we elect certain characters and they deserve to have a period of time to prove themselves. Those are ways to conceive of depending on the people alone, which I don't try to sort among. Whatever is good, I know that "dependent upon funders" is not.

At the end of the preface for Republic, Lost, *you wrote that you felt hopeful. Do you still?*

I feel more hopeful, because I think that we can begin to identify a form of social organization that is developing, enabled by infrastructure—technology like the network—and that has power and a capacity to reflect and to do something against the injustice or corruption of this existing system. When I was writing *Republic, Lost*, I wouldn't allow myself to have the belief in that because all we had seen was the Tea Party. As much as I respect parts of the Tea Party, I wasn't excited by it. But now you see Occupy and you see it standing next to the Tea Party and standing in line with a whole bunch of movements around the world, and you begin to see that these are all the same. They talk about themselves the same. There's a book coming out by the founders of the Tea Party Patriots that expressly says: We are an open-source movement. There's a "there" there and it could mature enough to actually do something positive. Not that it necessarily will or even likely will, but it could. And before, I didn't even see what that was or could be.

SAMPADA ARANKE

Sampada Aranke is a doctoral candidate in performance studies at the University of California, Davis. Her work addresses black aesthetics in the wake of black radical politics in the United States and the generative capacity of death and images of death during the Black Power era.

Aranke is what I would like to think a radical young person looks like: fierce, engaged, and adaptive, but with a sense of humor. "I have so much respect for dogmatic discipline," she told me, "but what we need is to translate it across experience and difference."

❦

Tell me about performance as a site of resistance.

Performance enacts and engages all of these really abstract concepts that we live out in our everyday life and magnifies them. When I teach my students about, let's say, embodiment—which is a concept that is crucial to performance studies, that centrality of the body—I ask, "What are the top five words you would use to describe me?" I'm a young woman of color and they all kind of tiptoe around race and gender and class, yet performance allows us to magnify those things, to see how our everyday experiences and our bodies and ourselves intersect with these large systems of power that otherwise seem so abstract or so distant—for some of us more than others, I should say. Performance allows for that kind of critical integration where the body isn't just some thing that happens after we think about things but something that's brought to the forefront as a site of struggle. Another thing I always tell my students is that we can't start resisting power until we name it, until we can say those things that are so uncomfortable for us to say, because then we can deconstruct it. And performance really puts all of those difficult nuances of everyday life under a magnifying glass.

When I think of performance, I think of artifice—so it's interesting that a practice involving artifice can bring us closer to what is real.

I think performance is filled with lies [laughs]. And I think that lies are the most powerful truths. I would go so far as to say that we try in every way possible or we're conditioned in every way possible to conceal the ways that we're connected through struggle. That's why the concept of solidarity is so powerful, this notion that, across difference, we are still in the same struggle towards an end and we're still connected in that way. Performance, I think, makes so much sense to us because it's based on an ultimate fiction and we are conditioned in our everyday lives as isolated individuals to also engage in those fictions. If I am a black woman trying to win an Oscar, I have to pretend that the roles I'm cast in are somewhat up to me, that I have agency in making those decisions. That's a fundamental lie that practitioners of a certain sort have to engage in, in order to make it in their performance world, yet those are the very roles or identities that are confirmed and rewarded. But that kind of foundational fiction is familiar to us, because we all make those sacrifices every day.

What was the point of inception of your political consciousness?

Everybody has those moments with teachers, don't they? One of my English teachers handed me a banned book, Assata Shakur's autobiography. Something happened in that moment where I realized the kind of conditions of oppression in a much more intimate way. The world I'd known had just been made sense of after reading this and I was starved for more of it.

It's always interesting how much political consciousness is activated, if not through direct experience, then through culture.

There's something it taps into and maybe this goes back to the idea of performance—or anything where you produce a work to be shared with others—which allows you to critically analyze experience. I'm not an artist or a practitioner in that sense but I think that in the moment of devising a work, no matter how much you try to run away from the personal of it, the practice of devising it allows you to make abstract connections more intimate.

Many people would say the same thing about participating in a movement.

It's that feeling of real consequences, that you're up against something in an overwhelming way. The minute you put your body on the line for your politics, in different capacities, that brings to light the consequences.

Has studying the radicalism of one particular group like the Black Panthers shown you that different groups are radical in specific ways?

I hold an unpopular stance on this question because I believe that blackness in America is kind of the ultimate threat. That's not to put everybody's suffering in some kind of hierarchy, but I do believe that because of the history of slavery and oppression in black communities, black positions in this country whether radical or otherwise hold a certain nugget of exceptionalism, for lack of a better term. Part of me believes wholeheartedly that when the Panthers called for nationalism, they really wanted a third world proletarian revolution and I believe that's something we can learn from as a basis for solidarity. But then another little part of me wants to think that there's something about being black in America that really enables, and yet forecloses, a lot of possibility within revolutionary struggles. Unfortunately, there are a lot of anti-black sentiments in progressive circles in the United States in subtle forms.

Are the conditions that produce radical behavior or reactionary movements specific to particular groups?

I think it's important for us to maintain specificity in that way because we haven't learned in our radical history that somehow difference always gets washed over.

Specificity can be helpful because it enables a degree of relativism. Things should not have to meet certain universal standards in order for people to feel that it's OK to want to react.

There is this idea that in order to "win" we have to be this homogenized blob, which usually always means a middle-class, white suburbia movement. Yet difference is our strength as we can create a shared language and vocabulary across class and language or experience or gender or race and try to struggle in those moments where we have to confront that difference. I think it's not about "winning" in the same way we think it is. We have those kind of small victories. The best example of this is the General Assembly model adopted by Occupy movements around the country, this tedious long meeting forum of direct democracy where you have to talk about every little thing. It's a fantastic practice because it tries to communicate across difference and show that any kind of revolutionary purpose takes work, and that that work is just as valuable—even more so—than maintaining the status quo.

What constitutes revolutionary behavior in America at this point in time?

I think that the kind of tensions that exist in this country are so preva-
lent—not just economic or financial but racial—and the right's assault
on women is a great example of this. But it's wound itself too tight and
I'm not quite sure what thread you have to pull in order for it to come
undone.

Although the implication there is that it will come undone at some point.

That's the part of me that believes that struggle is an inevitability. Occupy
is comprised of people who are struggling with unemployment, who are
angry at the financial institutional environment. Unfortunately we have
the Tea Party, which is one of the scariest collective organizing practices
I've ever seen, yet the root of that frustration can be seen as very similar—this frustration with the finances of the world being out of people's
hands. Yet, you know, I don't actually have hope that you can bring those
people to the other side.

*Although the presence of both does indicate that the conditions are right for
resistance, whether it's on the right or the left.*

It speaks to the urgency of the situation and the fear on both sides. What
I am fearful of is that the other side really might win. The more anarchist
tendencies in me love this polarized moment in U.S. history. It's really
bringing to bear contradictions about how both the right and the left are
invested in the same kinds of principles of capitalism and war—and not
providing for people's welfare. Part of me feels like, yes, that polarizing is
going to be productive because it's going to make something break, but
it also puts us in a precarious position because we don't have anything to
bank on. You're keeping your fingers crossed that it all pans out.

*Part of what people seem to agree on is that commitment is necessary regardless
of that ambiguity.*

Again, this is the anarchist in me, but that's what spontaneous organizing
is. Organizing isn't just this slog where you have to show up to meetings
every single day for the rest of your life. You're engaging in multiple and
diverse ways and when the moment is ripe, all of a sudden there is this
kind of burst. I think that is an organizing principle [Occupy] is based
on and that's why I feel that this is a spectacular moment in the United

States. There is a bridge drawn between politics and organizing and it's happening in these bursts, in these rupture moments, which I think is one of the most effective ways we can behave, for there to be something happening all the time.

It has that sense of presence and flexibility. It serves all of that rather than people feeling discouraged. The narrative that old models of social change give to revolution makes it hard for people to have faith in an unrecognizable model.

The narrative worked for so long because it paralleled the structure of power. As a lover of Marx, I think that his critique is taking moments or aspects or identity that have existed within capitalism, showing that contraction, and then organizing towards a principle of revolution, taking over the means of production, living collectively. My experience is that a lot of the people who share that narrative are old school Marxists and, I think, their reluctance of letting go of that particular idea comes out of denial that the system has changed so dramatically from 1972. Just with regard to the inception of what we know as neoliberalism and the privatization of everyday life, the narrative has changed so much.

I'm twenty-five. I'm not old enough to have seen the transition into neoliberalism. I've lived in it, so my tendencies tend to be similar to those folks who are organizing in more decentralized ways and in ways that are attacking all at once instead of just one thing at a time.

The means of production is a very abstract thing. It's not like I work in a widget factory and I can just take control of the things that make the widgets any more. Labor in itself is abstract and it's incredibly precarious. Technology has really fucked up the clear lines between when you're working and when you're not. For those of us who were born within that age, in that time period of technology, we don't know any other way but a decentralized way of organizing.

JEM COHEN

On the day of our interview, I walked with Jem Cohen while he filmed in the fresh snow. A train roared on the nearby overpass and a woman walked past holding a dry-cleaned shirt. Cohen filmed them both, and told me that what most people don't realize about his work is that it's actually quite funny.

Cohen is as engaged with what it means to document as he is with the act of documentation itself. His films include *Instrument*, about the punk band Fugazi, and *Evening's Civil Twilight in Empires of Tin*, which contrasts the decline of Germany's Habsburg Monarchy with present-day America. He has also made five so-called *Newsreels*, charting various stages of Occupy Wall Street in its first two months, with several more to be released.

How did you come to make Newsreels?

I went the first day of the proposed occupation, September 17th, with an old Super 8 camera, but shot very little footage. I'd gone out of curiosity and to support the event and it would be unlike me to go without documenting in some way. But as it turned out, it felt very disappointing—discouraging, really. It just seemed like the same old thing, protest-wise, and on a very small scale. I must have left, right before they settled at Zuccotti Park. But once that happened it all started to evolve very quickly.

A week later I shot some more Super 8 there, and then a bit of the October 5th march, this time in HD. I've mostly been a film person in the past [but] my shift to HD reflected some instinct that I might want to be able to turn the footage around quickly. Then this fellow who runs a movie theatre, the IFC in Manhattan, asked, "How are filmmakers taking this on, where are the newsreels?" And that really jumpstarted the series. I was already documenting but we got to talking and he said he might show them before movies, like old-time newsreels, which gave me a reason to dive in. I started banging them out, and at the same time I was getting increasingly hooked on what was happening with the movement.

What is the importance of documenting a movement? And, also, what are the problems?

To imply that there are problems? Well, of course there are. Two things that are somewhat inextricable in terms of what I was trying to do are: one, the urge to document—period, and two, the urge to be a participant and a supporter. By being there at all, I become a number for the head count and that's important to me. But being there with a camera gives me a job to do that I'm perhaps more comfortable with than marching in a crowd and maybe chanting a slogan, which, to be honest, can make me uncomfortable. Doing my work allows me to accomplish the two things at the same time. When I think about what I do, about documentation in general, there's some degree to which I just want to observe. I want to have my eyes and ears open and the camera can intensify that. I don't like to have a set plan or preordained intention, but of course I'm not a person without opinions. I have a point of view and strong feelings about the issues involved, so I wouldn't pretend for a minute that I'm subscribing to some proverbial objectivity. Suffice it to say there's a kind of dance going on between a certain kind of observation and emotional or political involvement.

You dedicate each Newsreel to a different filmmaker. It struck me that you are both acknowledging a tradition in filmmaking and acknowledging the historical recurrence of events that demand documentation of this sort.

I mean, Vertov is very different from Humphrey Jennings who is very different from Agnes Varda—but there is this recurrence, both in movements and films, and I think that's often oddly forgotten in the moment. The cynics reflect on this disdainfully by saying, "Oh, it's the '60s again." It's telling that the '60s are usually as far back as their sense of recurrence goes with regard to left-wing progressive movements. The less cynical among us might say this is the same *necessary* behavior recurring again and again, without which there would be a much more dire present.

We can look to the 1930s or the 1840s; to many, many periods in which there've been popular and unpopular uprisings, and then we see that these are absolutely crucial and that documenting them is a way of linking them, not in a trivial way but in a way that suggests this recurrent necessity. It's good for us to learn a little from the past so we don't have to reinvent the wheel each time.

I specifically chose filmmakers to dedicate these to who are fascinating and inspiring to me because they're politically engaged but not just propagandists. They were all, in a way, part of the movements they were documenting but they're not just taking cheap shots at the opposition or being simplistic about their comrades. Of course, I'm being simplistic now because—for example, the case of Dziga Vertov or Santiago Alvarez is very different from the other filmmakers. In a way they were propagandists, but they were also incredible artists, and Vertov eventually got into deep trouble because he wasn't capable of just toeing the party line. It might even be insulting to Vertov to say he wasn't a propagandist, but he was such a renegade and an inventor of a whole new language and he was so passionate that it carried him away from making films for the State in the language they would have preferred, for which he paid a heavy price.

Anyhow, the issue really is this recurrence, which can be both positive and disappointing. You sometimes think, "Oh my God, people are being so naïve and making the same mistakes that were made before," and you often see the left degenerate into internal arguments and back-biting and parsing degrees of theory and at its worst it can seem like what I've read about the Comintern meetings of the 1930s where people were not only losing traction but turning on each other. So all of that is problematic but it's also there to be learned from, if we have the documents.

Is it difficult to present impartial documentation when you feel affinity with the movement?

Since it's just me with the camera and I don't have a big crew to whom I can say, "Everyone go to a different corner and just observe," what I'm doing is making decisions constantly about what I think is interesting. Part of my doing that *is* as a supporter and an advocate. In one given minute on one given corner Occupy Wall Street could be extremely powerful and inspiring, or incredibly embarrassing and idiotic and misguided and confused. That's the nature of the beast, and I'm partly guiding my own vision, and other people's, towards elements that I think are genuinely interesting and powerful and, yes, progressive.

But then I try to temper that by also allowing in some things that are not so wonderful to me. And so I try to find a balance between that clarity I was talking about while also not ignoring that I want people to recognize that this movement is not just idiotic confusion. For example, when the weather was warmer there was a tremendous amount of attention in the media to the two or three women who saw fit to protest with their shirts off. My feeling about something like that, if it took place while I was shooting, was: Did I have to document it? No. In fact, I felt like the pendulum had swung way too far towards people being distracted by behavior which may have had some interesting reasons behind it but which was too easily misconstrued and, I think, a little irresponsible.

You know, if all the protestors could have been gathered together before they protested and brought to a fantastic film festival where they watched films from the '60s then they might see, well, yeah, there are hippies dancing naked in the mud and then there is something really important being said about the Vietnam War and it's OK to prioritize. When you're documenting, you have limitations of time and money and light and the focal length of the lens and you make decisions about what kind of balance to construct in your work. But again, my tendency would be towards saying, well, you don't pretend that these other things don't happen—you don't make it a matter of course to excise them—but you do make decisions about what is more important and then you concentrate on that.

I want to ask you at this point about Nineteen Hopes for an Activist Cinema.

Yeah, I wrote that a long time ago thinking about just these issues. Thinking about a tradition carried on by people like Chris Marker, certainly, that's thoughtful and complicating instead of thoughtless and oversimplifying, but that is still entirely charged with a sense of possibility and a sense of radical necessity. A lot of it has to do with the potential of filmmaking to help drop the veil.

So many of us are deeply fascinated by and indebted to Walter Benjamin, in part because of his proposition that the culture as a whole tends to sleepwalk. And that there are certain things that can sort of pull people out of that collective embalming, that collective coma. And you have to think about a way of doing that that doesn't condescend to the sleepers; that admits that we all sleepwalk, and doesn't just create an "us and them." I'm glad that *Adbusters* exists, they were a primary spark for Occupy Wall Street, but sometimes in the magazine I'm troubled by a tone of condescension and superiority and I think there are ways to recognize this societal slumbering without being disdainful or snide, and which also recognize it for the incredibly complex phenomena that it is.

I don't know my Marx all that well but if people are fair to him, they'll understand that he was actually capable of recognizing great complexity. He didn't just see capitalism as a monster, he saw it as something that people had to go through to get to someplace else, and he was capable—with extraordinary, original vision—to get at what was so problematic about that process. When Benjamin talks about the *flâneur*, he's talking about a new character on the stage of life; of people who are altered by walking around in, and looking at, cities. That can open up all kinds of possibilities but it can also make for laziness and for being hypnotized by the bright lights. He didn't make a simple designation about it and demonize or lionize this character.

But it's true that these kinds of movements can be so fraught. Benjamin sensed it when he went to witness revolutionary Russia. Some of the time I'm mortified. When you have an agora, when you have a genuine taste of democracy, you have a lot of people saying stuff you don't always agree with or feel good about or think is the smart thing to say. It's alternately inspiring and fascinating and awful. But one of the things about the moment of Occupy Wall Street is that at least it was there, at least it was possible, you just suddenly felt like, holy shit, there's this acre or whatever the dimensions are, where people *talk*. People actually try to work through some ideas, instead of just trying to get from the subway to the store to the refrigerator to the computer. This was remarkable and there needs to be proof of it. You make films not to boil that all down to just what felt good but to insist that people have the opportunity to be aware that it existed.

Even the oppression that came in response has its importance because, again, it lifts the veil. You realize that, basically, a bunch of people talking in a park is so worrisome that the authorities feel the need to respond with constant militarized readiness. You realize that these are real matters being brought up, that they are germane, or they wouldn't provoke such panic. There are different layers of reality but most of them we ignore out of convenience. That's what was so important about this movement: a positive inconveniencing, an unforeseen interruption.

What do you think it means to be active in the political sense?

I think you always have to be questioning the status quo, including the status quo of the side you're ostensibly on. If you're too comfortable in your beliefs, even if they're progressive, there can be something sedentary about that. When I look back at the people who inspire me, I look at people like Pasolini who, every once a while, lobbed a bomb that totally freaked out the left. I'm thinking of some comments that were not what people wanted to hear about the police in '68. He wanted people to remember that the police were also workers and that the college students who were yelling at them were sometimes dilettantes, which was extremely unpopular. Well, Pasolini was not speaking as an anti-intellectual right-winger—quite the opposite—but he said what he had to say and it shook people up.

But to get back to your question, I think to be active we have to be able to say, "Yes, it's all relative and we're all complicit and nobody's pure and wholly good," but then move from there towards making personal decisions about boundaries we don't wish to erase. One of the hardest places one can do that now is in terms of commerciality: [to question] what it means to succumb to a kind of increasing commercial takeover of daily life. We live in a time where a lot of people say, "There is no selling out and everybody needs to recognize that there are lots of different ways to be creative and we shouldn't be making old-fashioned distinctions," but I feel like, no, actually, there *are* some distinctions to be made. There is a difference between doing things primarily for sales reasons and doing things for some other reason; recognizing that there are actually territories that are in some way sacred, that there are languages other than commercial languages that need to be spoken which have always been spoken but need to be remembered and carried forwards. People have always made things for reasons of deep communication and out of inner need and out of the urge to surprise. I think all of that sometimes has to be removed from the sphere of marketing. And when people say that all creativity is one and the same and it doesn't really matter what the end game is, I think, no, actually, it matters. Again, how to find a way to talk about this without seeming superior and without being condescending is difficult, but I still think the discussion needs to be had.

People have really gotten sort of comfortable with the notion that the way humans interact is through trying to get each other to buy stuff. It sounds so naïve to put it that way but really, that's what it comes down to. And it dominates. It shunts other things farther and farther to the periphery to the point where people forget that they exist. I don't like when people hear me talking like this and think it means I am above that, because it's very, very difficult to get by in this world and I'm not so sure I won't ever do things that, to some degree, contradict what I'm saying. But at least I'll know [laughs]. At least I will try not to pretend.

Is it a question of awareness?

Well, it's awareness but you have to couple that with some kind of action. There are a lot of people who are aware but they are still like, "Yeah, I know, *but* you can't function without participating in that system." And then they often start to enjoy the participation. I'm not free of participating either, but at least I struggle with it and I try never to allow it to dominate the work. The *real* work. Every now and then I pay the bills with gigs where I shoot for something horrible but I see that as a depressing sideline, never the real function, never the real thing. I've tried to minimize it.

What do you think it means to be present?

I think that's an important question in the sense that I keep coming around to this notion of seeing things clearly or observing intensely. I do think that a lot of it has to do with being present. And the idea of being present has to do with that notion that when you try, to use the term I put out earlier, to "lift the veil," you are actually trying to recognize things as they are in a given moment. Not only recognizing certain layers of appearance, but also recognizing undercurrents and hidden structures and things that we might rather not think about. And when you're attempting that, you always have to be able to realign yourself to the world in its immediacy of light and weather and funny activity and, you know, all of the evidence there in that moment.

That's what this work, at its best, allows us to do. Film and photography in particular come with that inherent gift. It can even be too easy; it's not so difficult to make a *pretty good* photograph or film, but there is still this really wonderful capacity that they have to aid in being present, to take in the world in its many facets and to celebrate the things that are right in front of us. Sure, we mediate them and sure, we are guided this way and that by how we were brought up and what we learned and all kinds of things, but there is still this *is*-ness and to celebrate that is the core. And so this notion recurs again and again in different realms; we can see it coming from, say, a Buddhist direction or we can see it in a very beautiful way with regard to improvisation, when people talk of being unpredictably "in the moment" and therefore having the possibility of freedom. That to me is revolutionary, plain and simple.

MARTIN JAY

In a recent essay entitled "Mourning a Metaphor," in his *Essays from the Edge: Parerga and Paralipomena*, Martin Jay suggests a need to recognize the metaphor that underlies the concept of "revolution," which can alert us to the ways in which, "radical change often betokens restoration and repetition."

Jay is the Sidney Hellman Ehrman Professor of History at the University of California, Berkeley. His publications include *The Virtues of Mendacity: On Lying in Politics* and *Songs of Experience: Modern American and European Variations on a Universal Theme*.

Describe to me contemporary American society as you see it.

No one can see it from a vantage point above the fray, so any analysis of something as amorphous as American society would have to be partial and mediated by one's own concerns. I think that American society is undergoing what all dominant societies inevitably experience, which is an awkward transition to a different phase in its development. We are now adjusting to a world that went very quickly from the end of the Cold War, when we could imagine a future in our image, to one in which that narrative is in shambles. There is, of course, a certain amount of resistance to the diminution of our place in the world and comparative rank among nations. But although some still hold on to the image of the United States as a beacon to all of mankind, we have had to adjust to an increasingly more modest role. It's not clear that this is going to be an easy transition or that we're going to end up with a kind of equilibrium at the end of the game. It's also not clear that there are other societies out there that are going to provide a more inspirational model for the rest of humankind.

There's a well-known cartoon that I always like to describe to my history students in which Adam and Eve are leaving the Garden and Adam turns to Eve and says, "We live in an age of transition." Every seemingly static era is always in more or less rapid transit to something else. Ours may seem a bit more dramatic than others but there is never a period of absolute stasis or absolute satisfaction. There are always some groups that are anxious for change, while others are frightened by it. I would say we're in a period of normal rather than dramatic transition, and it is intriguing to wonder where it might go, if also a bit scary because of some of the negative potentials.

What potential do you see?

Economically, I think the smartest brains in the room have not come up with really good solutions to our systemic problems. I am not an economist myself so I can't suggest more plausible alternatives, but it looks as though we're really stumbling from one short term expedient to another. The larger global entanglement, which means that no economy is completely independent, suggests that there is potential for a larger level crisis than just within American society. That's the most frightening scenario. One can argue that, broadly speaking, capitalism always has crises and deals with them in ways that help some people and hurt others—but there comes a point in the development of any system where a crisis can't be successfully surmounted without the need for something significantly better, but also the potential for something much, much worse. I must admit that I'm not terribly optimistic about the former of these alternatives. I think things will get worse before they get better.

Is it possible to speak of useful ways to be political?

I'm a believer in the multiplicity of political actions. The people whose history I traced in the first part of my career, the Frankfurt School, were very keen to avoid turning politics into a utilitarian or pragmatic game in which everything had to have an immediate impact. They thought it was better, to cite [Theodor] Adorno's celebrated metaphor, to send messages in bottles to be read by people many years later and maybe acted upon in different, more favorable circumstances. That's one version of politics, in which one can be political without having a direct or immediate impact.

It's also true that one should think very soberly and with real responsibility about how your actions can make people's lives better in the here and now, understanding that "being political" is not just an abstract game in which you maintain your purity and become someone, as Sartre would have put it, with no hands rather than dirty hands, because you want to be above the fray. Sometimes you have to make hard choices, which may have an impact now, so being political in this sense means getting involved in more local and concrete activities. I've never myself felt temperamentally drawn to this type of sustained engagement, but I certainly respect it and think it's important. The *Virtues of Mendacity: On Lying in Politics* was, in a way, an indirect defense of people who do that and as a result sometimes compromise the moral imperative never to lie. Broadly speaking, they understand that political action and maintaining a "beautiful soul" may be in opposition, without necessarily turning politics into merely a struggle for power or advantage.

You have noted that the history of lying in politics dates back to Plato.

In *The Republic*, Plato made a plea for a lie that was noble enough to justify fooling large segments of the population. He was the first major philosophical theoretician of that nobility, understood not only as nobility of purpose, but also, in terms of the people who were doing the lying, who supposedly had noble characters and therefore could be disinterested enough to consider only the general good. Whether that was a delusion, of course, is another question—but it certainly goes back as a theoretical issue to Plato.

As a practical imperative, I'm sure rulers, leaders, or what we would later call politicians—not only in the ancient world that we know about, the Eastern Mediterranean, but around the world, where politics began in many different contexts—were similarly faced with the choice of whether or not to be realistic, effective, have consequences that are beneficial, or maintain their moral purity and follow what were moral or religious sanctions against mendacity. So I think while [lying] is an issue that was candidly articulated by Plato, other people were also struggling with it on a practical level.

You have noted that people make the assumption with regard to revolution that "without the promise of redemptive change, political activism will become a grey and uninspiring enterprise." I instinctively feel as though I want to defend a belief in redemptive change.

I think at a certain point we all are fed up with compromises and with small measures that produce only modest results and so have the hope that we can come up with a game-changing alternative. This might involve undermining a system or engaging in revolution; something that involves radical change, which may then bring about something more just involving real emancipation and maybe even tempting us to use a word which has as much religious resonance as "redemption." We sometimes are not satisfied with piecemeal reformist compromises, which don't really challenge the more fundamental structures and practices of our society.

But the history of seeking radical change and inadvertently producing bad consequences is cautionary. Nightmare politics can, we have learned, sometimes follow from utopian hopes. So in a world that is imperfect, a world where we're only fallible and understand that truth is plural rather than monolithic, and everybody has a right to his and her own opinion and the definition of his or her own interests, a world where it is only through coercion that we can assert a single truth or general interest, we have to be open-minded about the difficulties of achieving even modest change rather than yearning only for maximalist, redemptive change. This attitude may be a function of my getting older—it's a cliché that you get more cautious as you age—but I think you learn from experience that sometimes it's unwise to seek wholesale change because you end up with nothing. You have to be very careful not to create the conditions for a radical reversal of what you've already gained.

As imperfect as our society and our politics are, nonetheless, it could be much worse. We've gained certain things and created institutions that to some extent work for many people. To jeopardize those in the name of a blank check for a future that may or may not be brought about is something that I think we need to be very cautious about. The old cliché is still worth heeding: The best is the enemy of the good.

This is not to say that we should be cautious under all circumstances; sometimes you have to push for more radical change because, without it, things will basically remain the same and injustices will persevere. Occasionally you have to take that risk. There's no formula. It's an issue of political judgment where sometimes you conclude that the system is so intolerable and injustice is so rampant and the likelihood of reforming is so meager that you have to go for broke. But our own current situation, I think, is not at that point.

Are you suggesting that any point of decision with regard to radical action should be mediated by realism?

Occasionally realism is used to signal cynicism, to say all ideals and all critical positions are in vain and therefore one has to be basically accepting of a lousy situation. That is not what I mean. I think one has to be prudent and aware of the complexity of our situation. What Max Weber called the "Ethics of Responsibility," as opposed to the "Ethics of Ultimate Ends," meant you have to expect that your acts and your interventions may produce inadvertent consequences and you have to know that sometimes if you only go for the ultimate end, the ultimate value, you'll end up with either nothing or something that's the opposite of what you'd hoped for. Instead of maintaining the purity of your own position, you have to be aware that sometimes compromise [is necessary] to get at least partial results, which is better than no results at all.

In your essay, "Mourning a Metaphor," you argue for an awareness of the metaphoric nature of the word "revolution."

Often we assume we already know what we're talking about when we employ the concept of revolution. We have a few paradigmatic historical examples: the Puritan Revolution in seventeenth-century England, the French Revolution in the eighteenth century, failed revolutions like 1848 or 1905, and then more successful ones like 1917 in Russia or the Iranian revolution in 1979, even if some may argue the successful examples were ultimately betrayed.

There's also an underlying metaphorical dimension to the concept of revolution. As I pointed out in that piece, and this is not my own discovery, it originally meant a return and a restoration rather than a radical break, like the revolution of a planet in its orbit. Then it lost that meaning and became equivalent to a rupture in the gradual evolutionary course of history, indicating something radically and substantially different. Although the possibility of bringing about such changes by intentional action became an inspiration to self-conscious revolutionaries, there was nonetheless something left of the automatic working out of an objective process, like the revolution of celestial bodies in their orbits. The dialectic of objective conditions and subjective agency became increasingly apparent with each iteration of a new revolution.

Another issue is the threshold of substantive change that is necessary before various shifts in power or regime changes can justifiably be called revolutions. Was the American Revolution, for example, a "real" revolution? Although an imperial power was overthrown, there was not a lot of social change, so some have argued it wasn't one in the strongest sense of the term.

What we fail to do when we look at [revolution] only in these ways is to confront the non-conceptual residue of the original metaphor. What we learn by doing so is that we can't use the term as innocently and as glibly as we once did, because it can also involve a certain restoration of what preceded it. This is, of course, an argument that Tocqueville had already introduced in the case of the French Revolution, when he showed that it continued certain tendencies towards centralization and state-building in the *Ancien Régime*. Later revolutions may have claimed to be radically different but in fact often sustain as much as they innovate.

We're also in a situation where the very fantasy of a complete system change, even one like a kaleidoscope being shaken to produce a new constellation of existing elements, is extraordinarily hard to envisage. You can have a regime change, a change maybe of political types from a dictatorship to a democracy and so forth, but as we see, for example, in the history of post-Soviet Russia, there's an awful lot of continuity. Post-Soviet Russia is still authoritarian; there's virtually no public sphere that has emerged to challenge Putin's authority (or not at least until very recently and with what results we do not yet know). Of course, the Soviet Union itself, as many people have argued, preserved aspects of its autocratic Russian past. As a result of these kinds of experiences, it's very difficult to be naively hopeful about revolutions producing wholesale radical changes. Acknowledging the original metaphor allows us to see the return as well as the rupture.

Do you believe in the potential for the entirely new, or do you believe essentially in repetition?

I believe it's always an imperfect mixture of the two. There's no question that a lot of what seems to be new is basically a reshuffling of cards that have already been dealt. But having said that, I also believe that there is the possibility of radical rupture and newness. I've recently been looking at some of the discourse concerning "the event," which developed in France after 1968. One can give too much metaphysical weight to it, but the notion of the event is useful to signify something that brings about an unexpected and even unforeseen "impossibility," in the sense of not being understood as possible before it happens. But it does occur; something takes place that we did not expect, for example the fall of apartheid, the fall of communism, or 9/11. In hindsight, maybe we should have seen them coming, but we didn't. Even the economic collapse in 2008 had that quality, although a few isolated Cassandras had predicted it. So events do happen. Whether or not they then get folded back into the context out of which they emerged and become continuous with what preceded them, whether or not they initiate something that is very different and completely new, is not possible to know right away.

Hannah Arendt famously talked about the importance of natality, of birth, of the possibility that every individual who is born into the world brings at least the potential for change. We're born, of course, with attributes, with a gender, with a family background, with certain given talents and skills. We do not enter utterly *ex nihilo*; we're born with some baggage—but as we know, gender can be changed and potentials can be realized or not. There's a lot of breaking with tradition as well as reinforcing it. Every birth has the potential for creativity, and to that extent the past is not simply repeated in the future, but it is very sobering to see how often it is [repeated]. One of the things that is said about capitalism is that despite the surface stress on fashion, newness, innovation, constant change, on a deeper level there's repetition of the basic forms of the commodity, wage labor and the other things that define the capitalist system, so the system both needs rapid dynamism and has a strong static repetitive quality. The "ever-the-same" lurks beneath the surface of the seemingly new.

How does human nature stand up as a motivating factor in the desire to enact change?

One of the basic things that can be said about human nature, and this was Edmund Burke's point, is that artifice is man's nature. If you take seriously the idea that humans have an instinctual deficiency, which we have to make up through culture, then it is our nature to be culturally creative beings. It is our nature to invent different answers to the basic questions, which lead to different modes of behavior and systems of value. It is our nature to be diverse and plural, while at the same time we have the capacity to recognize a certain sameness in that difference, enough at least to say, "Yes, that is another human being, who deserves to be treated with dignity." Because of our primal inadequacy, we are always searching for answers that are never satisfactory to the most basic questions: Why am I here? How should I behave? What should I consider valuable? We don't have instinct to guide us, we don't have the simple repetition of patterns that are automatically produced in us, or at least we are not always ruled by the ones that seem to repeat regularly. We have the opportunity to reflect and be creative and, as a result, we are restless and can imagine that it could get better as well as fear that it could get worse.

Also—this is one of the most fascinating things that I think differentiates us from other animals—we feel a certain responsibility to posterity.

We understand somehow that there is continuity between generations; we try to recognize the claim of the past on us by honoring the victims of past injustices, but we also have a tremendous sense of obligation to the future. This duty to posterity creates a kind of restlessness. In most cases, we feel that we should add something to the world rather than simply take from it, and that generates a constant striving for something better in the future.

What did you think of Occupy Wall Street?

I was very heartened by it, especially after the Tea Party had seemed to get all the attention as the most active populist movement. I felt very alienated from [the Tea Party] because it seemed to be driven by resentment and a very shallow understanding of American politics and it had certain exclusive and even racist elements in it. The Occupy movement came at a time when populism no longer seemed to be available to the left, but succeeded in re-describing [populism] in terms that brought the issues of redistributive fairness and economic equality to the table. It also devised new and imaginative tactics to mobilize previously uninvolved people.

So I have felt, broadly speaking, a strong sympathy with the Occupy movement. As in all movements that have an anarchic and anti-authoritarian impulse, there were some people involved who did and said foolish things, but by and large I think it was—and still is—a very healthy development, which has had a healthy impact on changing the discourse of American politics. Of course, it's often said, and I have no answer to this, that the Occupy movement has been more negative and critical than it has been positive; it hasn't been institution building; it hasn't been focused on winning power; it doesn't really know what the next step is; it's not been able to really think about what needs to be done to provide cogent solutions to the problems it has identified. It's merely called attention to them—but maybe that's enough. Maybe somebody else, other people who play a different role, will in fact come up with constructive answers. But I was very heartened by the Occupy movement.

How relevant is creativity to what we're talking about?

"Creativity" is an open, perhaps even empty term, which we have to fill with specific content. At its most grandiose, it can suggest the human imitation of the Creator, who created something out of nothing, which is a great mystery. It implies that there was a Creator prior to that creation, which then always begs the question, who was the creator of the Creator? So it's a theological or philosophical conundrum. But I would say that this ideal of imitating the Creator, the idea that we can also be like the creator to some extent, is a significant spur to human ingenuity. However, unlike the Creator, we never create out of nothing: we have a menu of possibilities, we have a menu of likely innovations that are plausible under certain circumstances. Creation therefore is always in the context of what is possible rather than completely and totally out of nothing. Why some people are more creative and able to shuffle the cards in new ways and come up with radical new combinations is a great mystery. And if we take seriously the "impossibility" of events in the sense introduced earlier in our conversation, it may well be that interruptions in the smooth course of history are not so much created as witnessed and valorized, after they occur. We are perhaps not always as creative as we like to think.

JESSICA JACKSON HUTCHINS

I made a mistake when I assumed that Jessica Jackson Hutchins does not make political art.

Jackson Hutchins's sculptures—many of which are everyday objects made even more lived-in with fabrics or paint or the addition of ceramics—insist on recognition. In a time when we have many methods through which to distract ourselves from what is *right there*, Jackson Hutchins's works are an affront to our collective passivity.

For the Whitney Biennial 2010, she installed *Couch For a Long Time*, a sofa from her childhood living room plastered with news clippings of Barack Obama and literally occupied by a number of ceramic objects.

Jackson Hutchins has exhibited at the Institute for Contemporary Art, Philadelphia, the Seattle Art Museum, and the 11th Biennale de Lyon, among others, and is represented by Laurel Gitlin.

❦

You have said that your sculptures wouldn't be very interesting if they didn't also possess disruptive qualities and if they weren't tough and insistent.

I am in the middle of, and finishing, some pieces that are pretty new and I've had different people in my studio, because I moved to Berlin not that long ago. [The works] are a little bit confrontational and a little bit challenging and disorienting, and I noticed with people in my studio that if they don't really know the work, they don't really know how to handle themselves.

My own relationships to art objects and songs or novels or anything that has been really important to me are usually reliant on that kind of disruption that shocks me into a kind of recognition. It's not so easy to do something truly odd, to disorient in a formal way, because we look at so much. We're so steeped in images. I always want my work to have this humane, humble sort of quality because I was first and foremost against mastery and really aware of a power dynamic, not wanting to have a sense of heroics in my work but at the same time wanting to have something that is disruptive.

That disruption is a very political idea, and yet you don't make political work.

Oh, I think it's absolutely political and it was really consciously political for me. That position of mine was very much involved with power structures and the emancipation of the other, the radical. That's important to me, the Communist Project, but the radical emancipation of others. The way I approached it was very, very central to how I made my work and it was really about the relationship to the other.

Sometimes I think "political" is more to do with the elected powers that be or how the political system works or ideology, which is not the position that I am discussing with you now. It is related, but the emphasis is more on these power structures. They're everywhere, but I'm recognizing those and honoring or striving and ultimately thematizing some more ethical approach to the other in dialogue.

But do you say that you make political art?

Well, I wouldn't not. Some people call it feminist. That's not my agenda when I start off, it never was, but, yeah, of course it's feminist. If you want to read it as feminist, it's feminist. Yeah, it's political. I'm a mom, I'm an artist. Jesus Christ, that's not easy. I have to fight for every hour in the studio. I'm totally overworked as a mother. So I think being a woman and an artist and a mom is a political act.

You have spoken about the importance of the encounter as a way of knowing ourselves.

Experience is almost the only way I know anything. What I said seems so basic and simplistic, but it's just sort of beautiful to me how people read themselves and read other humans in everything. In one way the figure is so ubiquitous. You can't escape it. A chair in the room is a figure. Things are so anthropomorphized and we have this penchant to anthropomorphize things and that's ancient. We encounter objects and they tell us about ourselves, how we encounter them and how we read them and how we're always making sense of things around us. So many people do that and that is fascinating to me.

I feel as though, as society becomes increasingly atomized, the potential for encounter is lessened. Would you argue for a return to experience and encounter as a primary means of knowing?

That's how I live. I mean, I moved to Berlin because I just didn't know much about Germany. I have to sort of cram my face into it. I used to think a lot about the Impossibility. It's a beautiful thought, too, but through the impossibility of making oneself known and the distance between one and the other and the distance between the real and the symbolic . . . even as I'm saying that to you, it sounds tinged with a young person's hubris, right? Like [the idea of] an electable distance. But now I'm less interested in those distances and less convinced by them, and my experience shows how traversable they are and how much closer we all are than that.

You have also spoken about "encounter" as a word that suggests something that just is but that also has the potential to transform.

That is a little bit different because then the encounter is almost something that's happenstance. There's a poignancy and a humor in [that idea] which is attractive to me, where things just *are* but they also jump—maybe transform—into the symbolic: Something goes from a thing to a figure of speech to an allegory, even to a way of reading yourself and your life, and then right back to a thing.

I guess it's poignant because that idea is also grounded in everyday experience.

Right. It's poignant because there's a longing. It's all contingent on a longing, to recognize meaning in your life or to make sense of the moment or to help you articulate a change. Thematizing possibility and potential is very poignant and optimistic also. It's recognizing the reality of change. But that things have possibility is because we project that. We attribute use value and usefulness to something we talk about a lot. That's one reason I use ceramics, because I love how they are useful in the most mundane way. I like that you can drink out of my art objects even though you won't, probably. It's almost a metaphor for usefulness. Back to what I was talking about before, theoretical questioning is as important as your daily bread and in some cases more important.

Do you feel optimistic at the moment?

I have kids and in a way they make me optimistic. I'm not so pessimistic. In spite of overwhelming evidence, I'm not so pessimistic. I think I'm getting ready for the change. I don't think things can continue the way they are. Capitalism can't continue. It just can't. It will implode. I do think about it a lot, I mean I have to think about life daily, but besides that I do think about it. I think about my own complicity and my own pleasure in it.

I was reading a fairy tale to my daughters tonight, a very famous fairy tale about the twelve princesses. I've read it in ten different versions and in this one, every night the princesses dance their slippers to shreds so they need new slippers. There's a line in there where the king says, "It's getting too expensive to replace these slippers every day." That's so sick to me—the intrusion of capitalism into these symbolic slippers. But I like the [idea of] the "stop," because sometimes when you do nothing it's very violent, in that it invites change in a more significant way.

KURT ANDERSEN

Kurt Andersen is the author of several works of fiction and nonfiction including *Reset: How This Crisis Can Restore Our Values and Renew America*. He recently profiled "The Protestor" for the cover story of *Time* magazine's Person of the Year 2011.

I was most intrigued by a short opinion piece he wrote over a decade ago for the *New York Times* and, as he says, had not thought too much about until we spoke. The second paragraph of this essay, "The Next Big Dialectic," begins like this:

"At this end of this century, as we bask happily and stupidly in the glow of our absolute capitalist triumph, no long-range historical forecasters are considered more insanely wrong-headed than Karl Marx and Friedrich Engels."

The essay continues:

"The PC and the Internet begat a new fluidity of capital and information . . . which will surely beget some radical and infectious critique of this radically new order. In other words, the 21st century will have its Marx. This next great challenger of the governing ideological paradigm, this hypothetical cyber-Marx, is one of our children or grandchildren or great-grandchildren, and he or she could appear in Shandong Province or Cairo or San Bernardino County. By 2100, give or take a couple of decades, it's a good bet that free-market, private-property capitalism will be under siege once again."

Tell me about "The Next Big Dialectic." It is incredibly strange to read it now when people talk about the end of capitalism as we know it as a very real, or preferred, possibility.

I guess I'm more prescient than I know [laughs]. Well, I was then and remain skeptical of any historian, any person talking about history or the future, who suggests that it's all done now, that we've invented everything, that we understand everything.

I still think that at any given moment it's impossible to believe something like the present won't exist forever. But, you know, having lived more than a half century I have even more of a sense of the folly of that. Things I grew up thinking were forever, whether it's the "objectivity" of journalism or a kind of prosperous working class or that fundamentalist religion had disappeared from the main stage of the world and more specifically of the United States. . . . You know, I've seen enough things that seemed impossible, or issues that seemed settled as fundamental, almost existential issues, change. With "the end of history" and the triumph of liberal capitalism and all the rest of it, it seemed as though Marx and Engels and revolution were on the ash heap of history. But as a betting person, you're better off assuming that that's not the case.

Do you have greater belief in the potential for things that are entirely new or in the potential for renewal?

I wrote a piece recently for *Vanity Fair* about how it is strange to me that, for the last twenty years or so, so much of the material culture—the way cars look, the way people look, apart from technology, apart from our cell phones and computers—is shockingly unchanged. And [that sameness] is in a way that is not comparable to any other period for at least a century.

So there is a kind of frozenness on a certain level for a variety of reasons. I can't pretend to know all of them. I discovered this line that is attributed, maybe mistakenly, to Mark Twain: "History doesn't repeat itself, but it rhymes." I just found that to be one of the truest aphorisms I've ever come across, because that is exactly what it does. The idea of rhyming is to say, in important respects, it's kind of the same. Things do seem to rhyme, if not repeat, and it's an open question whether the United States of America has seen its best days or not; seen the peak of its cultural, political, or economic power in the world.

But this freeze, this stasis in so much of the culture, I really do think is strange and unprecedented in my lifetime. It's the lack of the new in these realms where, certainly, I grew up thinking newness was privileged above all else: literature, music, film, fashion, whatever. It no longer is. Things that are truly new are much more rare, so is that just a temporary thing? I don't know.

What do you think though?

As I said in the beginning, I'm so hesitant to say nothing will be new again. In terms of the political economy of the West, of the U.S., I grew up thinking that people work for a lifetime and then get good pensions and live a nice retirement. Well, that simply stopped being the case. If you'd said to the Americans of 1975 or '80, "By the way, in 2012 pensions are not going to be happening too much," they would've said, "What? That sounds horrible; that's dystopia."

I think as enough of those things get transformed and the social contract feels unfair to enough people, you do get revolutions. So I don't [see] something we would think of or call a "revolution" happening next year or five years from now, but I wouldn't say it's beyond the realm of possibility.

You wrote Reset *three years ago, but wrote more recently on your website: "Not everyone has taken advantage of the flux and new beginnings in the ways that I'd hoped."*

I thought that the terrifying "edge of the abyss" sense that I had, and certainly people I know had, at the end of 2008 and early 2009—"Whoa, we don't know what's going to happen next"—should've been and was terrifying enough to scare political people and political actors and citizens. I was naïve, not unlike Barack Obama, to imagine that. I still think some good things have come out of that terror, but I have come to think that maybe we didn't get scared enough.

It's an important question, whether bad situations motivate people more than the desire for something better.

Certainly, the myth—and by myth I don't mean lie or falsehood but the sort of self-defining myths that this country is so much about—is that we can make things good. We can make things better here, overseas, everywhere. A part of the frenzy and madness in our political life right now is the wishful repetition of that idea: This can be a great America. That was much easier to say and believe for most of my lifetime than it is today.

I think people still say it with greater hysteria than ever in a wish to believe it, but I think they know in different ways to different degrees on different days that, you know, maybe not. There's this repulsion at how different the United States of America is today than it was [at other times] within living memory. Do people really believe that this has been caused by a person who's been president for three years? I don't know. I don't think so. In their deepest, complicated hearts of hearts I think they understand it's a longer, bigger set of changes. But the anxiety and uncertainty is rife, so some people's reaction to that is to cling to things they believe irrationally. It's going to sound harsh, but I believe that's true whether it's certain kinds of religious faith or certain kinds of political faith.

One thing I say, and perhaps I said this in the book, I don't know: Yes, sure, we're polarized—but I look at the Supreme Court and if you compare how the person on the farthest right voted the year before last, and how the guy on the farthest left voted, they agreed. They voted together 60 percent of the time. I think it's a really important point that how Americans think about what ought to happen and what sort of country we are, the place where that is done most thoughtfully and seriously is in the Supreme Court of the United States. So it leads me to think maybe all is not lost, and maybe it's the best of times as well as the worst of times.

Do you think that your politics are by current definition "radical"?

No, I don't think so. Do you mean radical in that sense of radically left or going to the root of things and wishing for change?

I mean more the latter.

I don't know. Part of me is conservative but not in any way that's identifiably called "conservative" these days. Conservative in the old-fashioned sense: of worrying about revolutionary times and what can happen when everything is up for grabs and the tables are spilled over. You know, when the table is reset and things get back to whatever version of normal they get to, they can turn out bad. I spent a couple weeks last fall in Egypt and Tunisia and saw the good and bad that has happened there.

Part of me can understand that revolutions have to happen sometimes and they can be good. I take the long view, but you have to be careful what you wish for. So do I have radical inclinations too? Yeah, I suppose in certain ways. I don't know what the solution is to the problem of society not enjoying the benefits of automation and the rise of the machines. I'd be willing to consider radical solutions where that's the only way to reconstruct a system, or part of the system, but that's tempered by the need to be surgical about it. Let's be careful about this, even as we're doing this radical refashioning.

When we talk about resistance movements and revolution, what do you think constitutes success?

For one thing, I know it's rarely something to be judged quickly. I wrote this story in *Time* magazine in December about all the protests that had happened in 2011 and just gave a talk about it last night at the University of Connecticut. This student asked me, "So, about these revolutions in Tunisia and Egypt, are they more good than bad?" And my answer was what I just said: It's too early to make that judgment, but for now [they're] more successful than not.

These things are always messy in any short-term way—I mean anything short of at least five years. It's almost impossible to reckon success or not. I have a kind of simple-minded utilitarian Mill, Bentham view: Are more people benefiting than before, and were horrible crimes and oppressions and bloodshed mostly avoided? They're successful when it's better than it was before and not too much hell had to be paid in getting there.

One idea that seems to be discussed a lot is the necessary expression of discontentment. Is the actual occurrence of an uprising a success in itself?

Definitely it can be. Obviously Occupy Wall Street has not made a revolution in this country. However, what it has done already is not trivial in expressing a certain critique and a certain set of discontentments and in getting those discontentments—in the most basic terms, inequality and the corruption of the political system by money on the table—to be discussed and regarded by large numbers of people as important subjects.

I think there's purpose served by allowing people to figure out the nature of their discontent, or what they think the nature of their discontent is, and express it. Absolutely. In Egypt, some of the people involved in that revolution argue about whether this was a revolution or not. Mostly they say, yes, it was, but it's a problem with the word "revolution." The war on drugs, or the war on poverty, or the war on cancer—those aren't wars, but the semantic choice of calling them "wars" affects how people think about them and prosecute them.

Similarly, calling something a "revolution" is such a big, grand word that means a lot historically. If it's [about] getting rid of a dictator and his family and his associates, then the question becomes, well, what do we really mean by revolution? Going from an essentially nondemocratic form of government to an essentially democratic one is a big deal. But it may or may not constitute a revolution, because revolution means something different to each individual, really. The expectations met or expectations not fulfilled when that word gets thrown around can become its own problem in the aftermath.

SOL YURICK

On his refrigerator, Sol Yurick has taped a postcard of a work from the *Today Series* by conceptual artist On Kawara. It is an image of the date September 11.

Yurick is preoccupied with breaches to a false sense of security and he does not forget a thing, including the events of his childhood that fostered his radical perspective. His best-known novel, *The Warriors*, draws on the tragedy and farce of Greek mythology to present a picture of New York as a racially divided war zone.

Yurick's other published works include the novels *The Bag, Fertig,* and *Someone Just Like You,* as well as *Behold Metatron, the Recording Angel,* an essay addressing the philosophy and future of the electronic age.

***

You grew up in the Depression and have described it as "surreal craziness." What effect did that have on you?"

The crash that brought on the Depression took place in 1929. I was four. As I became aware of my parents being out of work, (we lived in a housing project which was an entirely communist enclave), there was so much that didn't make sense—I mean, to a kid. Always, there was the constant fear of not having enough to eat or being thrown out on the street. This was before a lot of the reforms that were passed by Roosevelt. I was sick a lot when I was a kid so I was more isolated and got socialized much later. To this day I look at the common interactions of people as if I was from a foreign planet, conducting some sort of sociological survey, wondering why people do the most ordinary things.

The traumas that you get, living in a state of constant fear, are the kind of traumas that are in Freud's category of traumas, and that partly shaped me. And also, my father being a communist and involved in strikes that sometimes turned violent, fighting with police, maybe the threat of his being hurt and that sense of hopelessness because you can't even really depend on your parents in times of extreme trouble. On the other hand, I don't think my father ever had a high school education but he could certainly read in three languages, Russian, Ukrainian, and English, and he was smart. He would find ways of explaining or giving a kid an economic analysis in the form of jokes. He took me places: to see opera, to see a production of Orson Welles' *Doctor Faustus*, which scared the hell out of me. He gave me Dickens' *A Tale of Two Cities* when I was ten, and I could read it. I couldn't understand a lot of it but I could read it. I don't remember my parents teaching me but I know by the time I was in sixth grade I was reading at a graduate college level.

The whole neighborhood was, for the most part, socialists, Trotsky-ites, communists. What was happening in Russia, we got the approved line. The purges were, at least for my father, real—or based on reality. I'd get all kinds of statements about the wonders of the Soviet Union, but my father was not dogmatic. He was a bit of a joker, which sometimes annoyed the apparatchiks. So there was this sense of being a bit different. My father was an uneducated smartest-boy-in-the-classroom, attended by the physical ability to beat people up. It was a question of survival. I remember stories about these strikes—these guys would cut police horses with their knives.

This seems to have been an education on certain human truths.

I'm trying to remember how it was being a kid. The teachers are trying to keep all those kids who come from leftist or communist families in school. Most of these kids were Jewish. I lived in a predominantly Jewish and Italian neighborhood. You know, you're being torn in two directions: wanting to be American and, on the other hand, resisting it and being a foreigner caught between a variety of worlds. I met somebody of my generation who came from a communist family and thought of himself as a communist, but who was a lawyer and wanted to be a Supreme Court judge. To me it's like, you want to destroy the system, why do you want to be a Supreme Court judge? It's that hovering in between.

In August 1939, after the Hitler-Stalin pact, I became completely disinterested in politics. I did not want to know from this business, because it was betrayal. So, here I am: I'm not comfortable living in a communist family because of the threats, I'm not comfortable being Jewish because I'm living in an anti-Semitic society and we're atheists. I was not Bar Mitzvah'd, even though my mother came from a religious background and was educated, which was very rare for Jewish women in the Soviet empire. There was this sense of being an outsider. There's this personal dimension as well as the ideological.

How did you come to pursue fiction and become interested in politics again?

I was a major in English literature—getting the whole picture, devoid of politics. At this point in time, there was no political or economic background to any of this stuff. I'm also doing the core curriculum: political science, history, almost entirely European history, and economics, the Samuelson variety. What I learned in this haphazard fashion was that I was already skeptical of any institution. I had to study for an economics final and I couldn't do it, it was too boring. And all of a sudden, I found myself once again trying to read all of Proust. Later on I made a connection, and this is a diversion but it's useful: What was the economic basis of Proust's ability to write this? The whole thing about sugar, Haitian slavery, wheat, the Paris Commune, Proust was born just around the time of the siege of Paris by the Germans, Balzac and the whole human comedy business. All this flowed together and the tie-in between the economics and the Proust became clear in my head. I began to see that one of the attacks to be made was on the whole ideological package underlying Western capitalism, and the same procedure can be done for all forms of domination.

Do you believe that symbols have inherent power? I would say that the theme of Fertig, as you have described it, "the destruction of the little man by the powerful elite," is a universal experience.

The symbols that are carried through by one group of people, yes, it means something to them. But introduce them to people within another system and it means nothing to them. When Marx talks about class, it's a level of abstraction too far. He's right, but the cultural and ideological content of class, makes the person who's in that class and not outside of it responsive. Marx did not take account of religious differences, national differences, local differences, which put a different spin on the relationship of people to the greater powers of their nation. The specificity has to be addressed if you want to change things. That was essentially the fault, in a sense, of the Soviet Union or Mao. They thought they could make the great leap forward in one generation. It couldn't be done. It had to be a long march, which somehow at the same time took cognizance of the potentiality for corruption of the leaders. It's a difficult problem in terms of revolution.

The question began to torment me more and more: The answer to Marx is that you can't change human nature. The Marxist reply is that there's no such thing as human nature, but I don't believe that. So my question was, is there such a thing as human nature? That has always been the critique of the right to the left. They can justify any kind of horror they want by saying, "This is what people do." But civilization is about restraint of the worst. It doesn't matter that this is what humans do; this is what humans have to be *stopped* from doing.

[Emmanuel] Levinas did an explication of some kind of Talmudic thinking and the point is that the bestial instincts have got to be tamped down. Bestial instincts are the ones that make life terrible for other people, as a result of what you do. This can be direct violence, and I think the urges are there although they are not in everybody, except under the direst circumstances, when people do terrible things. I'll give you a concrete example: Tiger Woods' wife has just demolished their Florida estate and is going to build a new one. Because of that, how many people are going to starve?

What led you to determine that there was such thing as human nature?

I found through histories and biographies that what people did was more bizarre, more violent, than anything I could imagine. When *The Bag* was a manuscript, I had a scene in it at the end where, after the ward is taken, it breaks out into an orgy. Boys, girls, everybody is drunk and screwing. My editor thought maybe it was going a little too far, but he left it up to me. I thought about it and cut it out. But later on, the more I found out, the truer it was. What I had reached out to through instinct, there it was [in reality]. The craziness is institutionalized worldwide.

In a sense, conspiracy is rampant everywhere, but it is natural. It starts in kindergarten when one set of kids gets together and pushes out another set of kids. The structures of how power develops and is implemented, whether you're talking straight politics or criminal activities, corporate activities . . . I see the same kind of structures from tribes to great States, I don't care how far back in history. There must be something biological if everybody is doing the same kind of thing. Everything is in flux, nothing is rigid, but there are certain patterns that repeat. Once you see that, you begin to know what the problem is. I mean, for instance, to try to describe the United States power structure is an enormously complicated thing, but you can also say that it is a consortium of interlocking oligarchies.

During the days of the '60s, when a lot of the kids were discovering Marx for the first time, their idea of the ruling class was that it was always in agreement and always knew what its ideology was going to be and how to behave. No. [The ruling class] will fight each other to the death but everybody else pays the price. So if this recurs in a species, you have to say there's something biological motivating it, although there are always significant exceptions, because biology is not mathematics.

Is there a distinction between political behavior and human nature?

I think political behavior is human nature carried on within certain social restrictions. But again, I'm not saying that every segment of the human population is power-driven. There are people who seem to need to be ruled by power.

In a sense, to go back over the whole question of making a social revolution overnight and why it can't really be done, and certainly can't be done by people who are purely intellectual, you've also got to have an idea of what happens on the ground and how change is affected. In the 1980s, it began to puzzle me how an American or British public relations guy can go into an African nation and help win an election. But they had one piece of knowledge: They knew that people had wants, but they knew that they couldn't promise the satisfaction of those wants in terms of the society they came from. It was a question of finding what symbols, what promises, would move these people couched in a particular language. If you gain control, how do you break down those ties? How do you break down the contempt that the Russians had for the Ukrainians? You can't do it fast, but if you can maintain control then you can do it.

What is the relationship between literature and social change?

Did you ever read *In Cold Blood*? It starts off with the murder and really raises the question of whether Clutter had it coming to him. When I wrote a review of Capote's book for *The Nation*, I had an inherent hostility to [Clutter] before I remembered exactly who he was. Then I remembered I had read a piece about Clutter in the *New York Times*' magazine section in 1954. It was about a big change taking place in American agriculture and the perennial question of how to deal with overproduction, because how do you make profit on overproduction? And the spokesperson was Clutter. Is this an instance of the tradition of the perpetuation of class injuries, not only to yourself but all the way back to myths and mythology? It brings up the story of Joseph in Egypt. The first year, the peasants come to Joseph wanting grain and he says: Give me your money and I will give you grain. The second year, he says: Give me your cattle. The third year, he takes their land and moves them into the cities and he's selling grain on the world market. There are shades here of the Soviet Union. The people were starving and they were selling grain on the world market. The same thing happens in the United States. There comes the efficacy, I think, of tying the mythology and the practical together but also writing about it in an imaginative way.

Speaking very broadly, what potential do you see for change?

First of all, I think a lot of changes are coming at the moment but they're coming from the right. The reinvigoration of religion, the gradual destruction of government—government will exist only as an adjunct for corporations—and at the same time, an increase in internationalism on top levels and nationalism on bottom levels. More than that, I think one of the most serious political and economic forms that has to be addressed is the growing rate of organized crime groupings. Those are real political forces. They're not negligible, they're major. And all of this is behind a threat of the total collapse of the environmental system and, over the next few years, a real threat to human life, not to mention other forms of life. The kind of revolution that we like to talk about, I don't see happening. I don't see why people look to China. It's a fascist country and a police state, and on the lowest level a combination of police and crooks. I'm not sanguine, I think there will be uprisings everywhere but there are thousands of little uprisings in China every year and it's making people on top levels nervous but they're not adjusting for it.

Do you see any positive potential?

Not now, I really don't. I'd like to but I don't. In a certain way, the course that the information revolution has taken is, for the most part, distracting. As I like to phrase it, you've got more and more people circulating more and more capital at faster rates. You've got more and more people cut off from any sort of economic activity and they're never going to climb up. There's no room. I don't see anybody altering in any significant proportion their habits. And it's depressing. The Occupy movement I think is good and it should happen.

What is the power of understanding history?

Well, for me, one of the absurdities that I realized at a young age is—at a very young age, I asked my father, "What happens after you die?" and he said, "Nothing." This was very disturbing and had an effect on my life ever since. In some sense, I grope toward understanding where I am in the universe and why. But there really is no why, I think. So [history] becomes to me like a search, like I am going to discover something really new. When I was younger, the library saved my life because I couldn't afford books. I would have this dream, and I still have it now and then, that I would discover a library with all kinds of books that I'd never imagined, and in a sense the books were like a lifeline out of this existence.

I try to imagine what it is to not exist and there being no "you" to know you don't exist. I mean, the nearest I can come to it is like having been under an anesthetic or when I had my first bout with cancer, I lost about a week entirely with irretrievable consciousness of what had happened to me during that week. That was the closest I came to nonexistence. I am not saying this is for everybody. I like the stories, too. There are whole areas of history—I've read a lot of specialist stuff trying to find out what did and did not work—so you know, just exactly what power struggles took place within a particular Chinese emperor's reign. What was the purpose? What power did the eunuchs have? I want the kind of concreteness you actually don't get. It's like a hunting, and also as I say it's a hunting for stories. Because besides the fact that I would write them and rewrite them, I still like to read them.

KEVIN KILLIAN

Kevin Killian, a poet, playwright, and author, was once described to me as a "cornerstone" of the San Francisco arts scene. Indeed, Killian has witnessed many definitive moments in the city's recent history. The AIDS epidemic, in particular, was the impetus for a volume of poetry on the films of Dario Argento, *Argento Series*. At the end of the book's introduction, Killian explicates the unique confusion of witnessing horror: "I saw something important I can't remember."

Killian has noted, "I began writing the poems of *Argento Series* at a time when I had despaired about ever finding a vehicle that would convey something of the socio-political issues around AIDS that had come to preoccupy me to the extent that nothing else in life seemed worth doing if it wasn't contributing to the war on AIDS. How could any writing move into the realms of horror and disgust we were confronting every day?"

Killian's published works also include *I Cry Like a Baby* and *Poet Be Like God*, a biography of Jack Spicer and "the San Francisco renaissance," co-authored with Lewis Ellingham.

***

What do you see when you look at American society?

I'm in despair in a way. I'm glad I won't be around much longer to see the end of what's going to be happening. I'm in my fifties so I think by the time another fifty years goes by, it will be hell on earth. It's hard to say exactly what I'm talking about, but I feel like the whole country is under control of just a few people. I don't even know if they know what they're doing, but they're owning every speck of it. There's no free space, there's no place to be. Every moment on earth, we're paying for the privilege of living here, and somebody is making money out of it. I mean, I suppose

I'm making money—that's how I live, by exploiting other people. But even in the course of my lifetime it's gotten much worse.

If I'd asked you that question maybe thirty years ago, what would you have said?

I remember being a kid during the Youthquake. We protested all the time, we were angry. When Lyndon Johnson was president and Richard Nixon was president, I thought it couldn't get any worse. It was like being in a fascist state. Today, even with all the hideous right-wing rhetoric we have to listen to night and day, things aren't quite at that level. It's just a pervasive knowledge that things are being controlled by a twisted capitalism that's destroying itself, eating itself from within. I would never have children today. Never. My friends are having children, and I don't say it but I don't think those children will live a full life.

What is missing?

I think that people should have more of an education and in, say, political theory, economic theory. They should know about money and they should investigate their own sense of nationalism. I guess every country in the world has its own version of a patriotic feeling that if you're from here you're protected, in order to distract you from the globalization that owns everything.

Tell me why you haven't given up.

Well, I think we're still here on earth to lessen the sufferings of others, to have compassion. There must be other plans for our planet. I don't know what they could possibly be. Maybe I'm exaggerating about how bad things are but I just think that there's not going to be any air, there's not going to be any water, there's not going to be any soil.

I've been reading a lot of Samuel Beckett. He was about: What's the point in going on? Life is all about: You grow up, you try and you fail and you try again and you fail again, then you try again and you fail better. But also little individual victories and pressures are enough to keep me going. I think they probably are for most people and they always will be.

I also think that being a writer and an artist I can change the way people think. It's not like I have it all worked out and I have the answers, but I think that I have more agency than, say, other people in my office. There's maybe eighty of us, a white collar type of setup, and I'll say, "What did you do last night?" and often they just went home and watched TV.

But it's not even that. They just work, work, work and do absolutely nothing else. It's very bizarre, so I feel like I'm more alive than they are. But maybe that's just bullshit.

Has there been a time when you have witnessed people taking initiative to circumvent or stop a bad situation?

The direct action against AIDS I think really changed things. It saved the lives of 100 million people. So that did happen because of people, activists and so on. There have been a number of great victories. When we had our Occupy Wall Street [in San Francisco] some of my friends, especially my young friends who are in their twenties, were saying that, being out on the streets and protesting, they had never felt as alive. Wordsworth said in the *Lyrical Ballads*, "Bliss was it in that dawn to be alive but to be young was very heaven." I really did feel like Tiresias.

What did you observe that mobilized people?

Maybe people feel great passion and they feel outrage, they feel they're being ignored. There's great strength in camaraderie, in finding others like you. That's what the right wing also depend on, this gathering together of masses of people who are upset, angry, outraged at what they see. They feel passionate enough about it to make great changes.

Do you still believe that it's powerful to articulate discontent?

That it's powerful? I guess you're exercising your own power of speech, yeah. It's not like I'm a Buddhist or something like that, where it's all going to pass, nothing matters. And I think the Occupy movement is especially impressive when I consider how young people in America have so little to look forward to, they seem so dead in many ways, but were able to wake up. It was almost like dead people coming to life. And maybe when you have a resurrection like that you don't go back to your state of ignorance.

At the end of your introduction to Argento Series, *you wrote: "I saw something important I can't remember."*

If you've seen Argento's films that's the line that most of the heroines, sometimes the heroes, use. They saw what happened but they can't put their finger on what it was. That was the feeling I had with AIDS, that it kind of slipped by me, it slipped into existence and I must have seen how it all happened but I just couldn't remember. Part of it was my own, you know, doping and drinking and sexual abandon—but also maybe there wasn't anything there to see. I kept thinking, maybe it's some kind of terrorist plot to destroy gay people. But I don't really think it was. Maybe it was a mistake or just nature acting out. So when I heard that line in the movie I thought, yeah, that's how I'm feeling about AIDS. I think it's also true of how I'm feeling about neoliberal verbalism. It just arrived and I didn't see it coming.

Tell me about trying to contend with life through art, through poetry.

I only recently realized why I had come to California. I thought it was that I left a graduate program in New York to come here, to abandon my dissertation, to become an office worker, well, really a creative writer, because there were so many cute guys here. But I realized I'm not really a writer or a poet. I'm an artist. And I'm this particular kind of California artist where it's all about contingency and it's about imperfection and it's about failure and it's about things disintegrating. What you make is going to be dissolving. After I realized that I said to myself, "You've wasted a lot of time just trying to make every sentence perfect, and it's not about making things perfect. It's just about trying." It's about making the gesture.

Perhaps creative work is able to address ambiguity in a way that other conversation and discourse is not.

As I get older, I find myself drawn more to agitprop, to actually ignoring ambiguity. I'm doing a freeform interview with a magazine editor that has been going on for a year. One of his questions was, "What's the kind of art that you haven't made yet?" Another question was, "What's the kind of fiction that hasn't been written?" I was trying to think of what it would be and, really, it would be a writing of persuasion. Although, it's not that narrative hasn't been used by all the wrong people. They say it was no accident that the novel grew in bourgeoisie society once the Industrial Revolution began, that it became where the bourgeoisie found its mirror.

I guess I could have an anti-novel, something that would persuade people to just break it all up, to break down society. I do admire that, I do admire revolutionary writing, revolutionary art. That's what I'd like to do but I don't know if I could. I'm too ironic, or maybe too sincere. Maybe you can't want something to happen that badly and expect it to work. Most revolutionary art should probably be accidental.

CANDACE FALK

When Candace Falk speaks, she draws as much from her own experience in the women's and antiwar movements in the '60s as from the life of another: "Red" Emma Goldman, the late nineteenth and early twentieth century anarchist and activist. This duality of political engagement, the personal and the historical, renders both stories surprisingly contemporary.

As the founder of the *Emma Goldman Papers* at University of California, Berkeley, Falk has worked to publish dozens of essays and several books, including *Emma Goldman: A Documentary Edition of the American Years*, which spans four volumes. Falk is a Guggenheim fellow and has received multiple awards and nominations for her work as a historian and a writer.

***

What would you consider to be your first political experience?

There are a lot of ways to define "political" but I guess the most direct experience that I had was when I was an Arts Humanities major at the University of Chicago. I was aware of politics but also went to a school that was very engaged with the life of the mind. During the time of the Vietnam War, friends of mine were either being drafted or doing draft counseling and at the same time Martin Luther King was shot. I was in Chicago and a good friend of mine was working at the library across the Midway, which, at the time, was the median strip between the university and more of what you might call the African American ghetto. As he was walking home from work, someone shot him and he died. And that was some kind of incredible wake-up call to me that someone would shoot someone they didn't know, because he was white and walking across the median. But then I started to understand things about racism and the anger after the death of Martin Luther King, and linking it to the war in Vietnam. So I came to [politics] out of incredible sadness, and trying to understand that. I think in some ways when you have a visceral experience your commitment comes from a different place.

It was a certain time in history. When I went back to Chicago to do my master's degree I was determined not to split the life of the mind from the life of the community and the people. My interests changed, but I was still very hooked onto the humanities. A lot of what I did was be what one would call "extracurricular." I joined a group to study Marx with all these really brilliant people. I joined a women's group that was interested in international issues as well. Those people became the people I trusted most. I felt like there was more substance there. It wasn't that I didn't take myself seriously as a student, but I took myself more seriously as a citizen of the world.

There was a meeting where Vietnamese women came to meet with people from the U.S. women's movement but couldn't come to the United States, so they went to Toronto. We needed a representative of the women's movement in Toronto and I became that representative. It was odd to be a representative when clearly nobody was. I remember we decorated a hall with flowers and welcoming things, and then one person in our group said, "These women have gone through war, we should take down our decorations, this is really serious," so we took down our decorations. Then when the women came up on the platform the first thing they did was sing a song, and we felt ridiculous. We felt like we didn't understand the combination of art and the affirmation of life in the middle of terrible sorrow.

When I was at the University of Chicago we read nothing of women's writings and definitely nothing of political women's writings. But Emma Goldman's autobiography had been reissued. Her biography was written in 1931 but it was very much about someone who lived her politics, and we all loved it. When I went on to teach in southern New Jersey and lived by myself on this little island, I got a dog at a pound, a red Irish setter and I named her Emma: Red Emma Goldman.

How did you come to incorporate Emma Goldman in your academic work?

I felt beholden to write something with respect about the relationship between her public and personal lives. It was the era of "the personal is political," so I began to write about those issues. Also, at that time, which is interesting in terms of the Occupy movement and my own evolution,

I was critical of what I thought was a much-too-rigid vision of the way the world should be: everything harmonious, and so on. I felt that was an entire movement set up for constant disappointment.

I felt that Emma tried to live as an example, which was what gave me the feeling that it was OK to write about her because it was a political statement. A lot of political figures don't want their life to become the subject of politics but she really did. So there was a kind of critique in the volume, I ended up following all her different relationships trying to get at her through a different lens, trying to solve the issue of how you keep your vision but drop your illusions.

What is the significance of Emma Goldman as a figure?

Anybody who works on one figure for a long time often finds different facets that are important at a different time, and all together they make one composite person. Early on, I was fascinated by the level of passion that she had both politically and personally. There was something wonderful about affirming intimacy as part of politics. These images of grey-suited communists being ultra-purist didn't appeal to me. The project and also my sense of Emma Goldman started from a very feminist place: a woman who stood against the tide. It was almost more abstract, and her anarchism was part of a beautiful vision that I related to but which took me a long time working on the papers and on the whole [anarchist] movement—we have 20,000 documents that we've collected and another 20,000 from doing the volumes—to understand. I now have a much larger appreciation for what that movement stood for and what Emma Goldman stood for.

The way I see her is as somebody who stood fast to the idea that it made a difference to articulate the horrors of inequality; to see the way a government that's linked up to capitalist greed can't get out of that entanglement. She lived in a time of incredible reform, there were great things that were happening with sanitation, schools, penal laws, but she felt like all of these things were Band-Aids, and in some ways turned her back. She felt like it was the liberal vision that reform would make a difference, and she felt like what was needed was a true trans-valuation of values.

A lot of her life was based on educating people about what was possible. Many who came to her lectures or read her magazine, *Mother Earth*, couldn't live out what she spoke of but loved imagining that kind of freedom. Women would come with their baby strollers and hear about how love and marriage didn't always go together and that marriage very often was a property contract. When people would accuse her of not being realistic, she would say . . . here's something she said in 1901: "As long as I live, I must be a crusader. What I think, what I feel, I must speak. Not for a hundred, not for five hundred years perhaps, will the principles of anarchy triumph. But what does that have to do with it? . . . It is the touchstone of courage and principle."

I feel, for example, when I see the conversation switching with the Occupy movement, that Emma Goldman could have been right in the middle of it as someone who would have felt completely in sync with the non-hierarchical way of dealing with things, with the vision of direct action with standing up for the poor and identifying as a whole culture as well as internationally. She always believed that free speech and economic struggles all over the world were related, that we were all connected, and that that was part of the anarchist vision. I think any revolutionary, any visionary, any dreamer or iconoclast is fated to be misunderstood and that theirs is a lonely life.

It is said that principles don't exist in a vacuum. What conditions give rise to convictions as strong as that?

For better or for worse, the 99 percent notion of tremendous inequality of economics and opportunity really does set the conditions for people to understand things they might have been shielded from before. [Before] they could sit back and say, "We're middle class and we're not struggling *that* much," and they could put a shield between themselves and the really poor and really struggling. It's not the same anymore.

From 1910 to 1916, the receptivity to Emma Goldman also had to do with the conditions. People were more open. And it goes both ways: On the one hand, dire conditions can limit one to wanting the basics of food and shelter. Sometimes people who are in that situation have a hard time going beyond that because they don't have a choice. So there's a creeping level of privilege that gives people the freedom to imagine. Now, many people had the image that they could go to college and get a job and grow up not struggling, and it's not true in the same way except for a small percentage of people.

I think a lot of people identified with the Occupy movement but were too afraid to say. The core values are human core values that people relate to all over the world. That is what is most moving to me. Having lived through different movements, I often feel as though right before a movement people think nothing is going to change. A year ago, people were forlorn. That's why we have this quote on our holiday card: "How powerful is the ideal sweeping across space and time, knitting people together into one great, sweet comradeship."

And this is integral to Emma and to anarchist politics: Things develop out of certain conditions, and the conditions that would create one kind of structure at one point in time do not create the same structure at another point in time, and it's not for me to say what that structure should be. Having it come out of a group process, and gradually, is much more meaningful. I'm not a seer but the advantage of working so much in history is that you can see patterns. In 1901, when President McKinley was shot by somebody they thought was an anarchist and the nation was in fear, all of a sudden the conservatives had free reign to put in place terrible, repressive laws. That was the first time people were kept out of the United States based on their ideas.

This is a very difficult economic time all around and a very difficult time to get a grip on how to do life. When so many people have taken advantage of the system it's a good time for something to change, for people to want to make change. There is always the caveat that you hope things don't get crushed, but I don't think anybody can ever crush this moment of optimism. Whatever happens, it can't go away as part of our history. In a way, working on the papers of somebody who was deported based on thinking that no one should go to war without wanting to . . . she suffered for it but her speeches, her statements to the trials, are so moving and seem so contemporary. And so I am trying to figure out how to make sure that history is not deported as well.

JULIA BACHA

In 2003, shortly after America invaded Iraq and Julia Bacha had completed her undergraduate studies at Columbia, she was accepted into a master's program at Tehran University. Unable to get an Iranian visa as an American, she was advised to enter another Arab country where her Brazilian nationality would expedite the process. She went to Egypt, ostensibly to work with director Jehane Noujaim as she filmed inside the newsrooms of Al Jazeera. That film became the documentary *Control Room*.

Bacha has directed two feature-length documentaries, *Encounter Point* and *Budrus*. The latter tracked a ten-month nonviolent protest by the residents of the titular town in Palestine, protesting an Israeli West Bank barrier scheduled to be built through their village.

You often refer to the lack of coverage that nonviolence receives in mainstream media. It occurred to me that this is because spectacle has become fused with our idea of protest.

There's both a general challenge that media faces in terms of what kind of stories it chooses to cover and a specific challenge related to the time we're living in right now. The general one is that there's an ongoing conversation between the producers of media outlets and the consumers. I think there is a tendency among consumers, because they have less and less time, to focus on simple, sensationalist stories. The media reinforces it by only giving them these stories. There isn't intent, and there's no funding for investigative journalism. There's a failure in that kind of business model because it emphasizes what's short and fast.

Something like a nonviolent resistance movement is not something that has results fast and it's not as easily captured in a single picture, specifically in the context of Israel and Palestine. If there's a car bombing, it's a very simple thing for the media to cover. They just have to get one picture of the car. You can plaster that on a front page, everybody will understand why it's there and people are going to buy the newspaper to read about it and there's going to be outrage. This makes it easy both for the media to feel like it's fulfilling its role and for consumers to also feel satisfied. Nonviolent resistance and any form of civil disobedience is usually not as—to use the term ironically—glamorous as a terrorist attack. For you to cover a long-term protest in a way that will awe people, in a way that will sell newspapers, you need to invest time and money in a reporter spending the necessary time to win the trust of individuals on the ground so they can actually tell the story in a compelling way. Also it requires a little bit more creativity, and I think there's less and less creativity involved in journalism because it's not being demanded as much anymore. The creativity now goes into entertaining people through media.

It's not anybody's fault but it's everybody's fault, which is a challenge because it's systemic and this is where we are right now. I have seen firsthand many times, that consumers are hungry for these kinds of stories and I know journalists are eager to tell these kinds of stories.

What is the difference between documenting a movement and advocacy filmmaking?

I've been making documentaries for ten years and, from the get-go, that was a big question. In a very personal way, I didn't enter into documentary filmmaking as a passion originally. I always admired films, I always loved documentaries, but I never thought it would be viable as a career. The moment I looked at the footage Jehane Noujaim shot inside Al Jazeera, I was blown away. This was 250 hours of primary source footage in real time. There were interviews with the Al Jazeera journalists and the Western journalists posted on Central Command, which was the U.S. media and military headquarters during the war. I was completely blown away with the possibility of working with this material in putting together a story. And that's when I realized that I could do what I wanted to do with a potentially much bigger audience. Of course I had no idea what the documentary was going to become in the end. The film was made very much on a shoestring budget, and it became one of the highest grossing political documentaries in the U.S. That really opened my mind to the possibility of documentary and the power of filmmaking as a medium.

There's no question that I'm a very conscious person in terms of making sure that I do my best to be aware of my biases, that I am not going to be manipulating footage or angling things toward one side or the other. But there's also no question that the reason why I'm doing this work in the first place is because I want to change the world. That will inform a lot of things, even on a subjective, unconscious level. So [the question of documentation versus advocacy] needs to be constantly in the back of my mind. In a very practical way, which I think holds me accountable and makes me feel less anxious about those questions of objectivity and accuracy. I've made a commitment to myself that I will always show my films to the people I shoot and usually that includes people from both sides.

In the case of *Budrus*, Israel and Palestine, one of my main characters was Yasmine Levy who is an Israeli, former Magav, which is a combat unit, the Border Police in Israel. She's someone who's very open, but her position in the film is a complicated one. It was important for me to be honest about who she was and not in any way try to use her character to make a point about anything. I think I helped myself through this commitment that I have, since the time of *Control Room*, to show the film to the characters. In *Control Room*, I wasn't the director, I was just the co-writer and editor, but ever since I've become a director, that has been one of the guiding principles for me. And I have a very good track record with people of all kinds of backgrounds watching the film and feeling like I gave an accurate portrayal of who they are, which was what Yasmine said about the film.

One of the protestors in the film says: "We must empty our minds of traditional methods." This is a very powerful idea.

Something that often comes up is that people say, "Oh, this is the first time Israelis and Palestinians are using nonviolence," but it's not true. There is a very long history of nonviolent resistance in Palestine, the First Intifada being the biggest example of that. In many ways, [the residents of Budrus] were employing a lot of the tactics and tools that they had used. The speaker you're referring to was one of the leaders during the Intifada.

But the big leap there is the traditional context under which you assume you're operating. This means so many different things: that Israelis are all enemies, they completely broke that tradition; that women can't demonstrate: they broke that stigma; that Hamas are bad people, none of that, we're going to work together. These ideas somehow get stuck in our heads and we don't realize that we're being ruled by invisible norms. We just think that's the way the world is.

I was reading about this experiment where cats were raised in two different environments. One group of cats was raised in a room that had only vertical lines and the other group of cats was raised in a room that had only horizontal lines. After years, they were put in a regular environment. The cats raised on horizontal lines were great at navigating but couldn't identify the idea of jumping up on a table because they couldn't see verticals, whereas the cats raised in a vertical setting were very good at jumping on top of things but they kept bumping into everything in front of them. For me, that is so telling of human beings as well. We are raised to see things in particular ways. And I think that's where I am constantly trying to operate: It's not stating something new necessarily, it's showing people what has been in front of them the whole time.

I have read that the film you are most inspired by is The Battle of Algiers. *This is interesting because it's a good example of how narrative can reflect some of the complexity and nuance of real life.*

I think storytelling is very powerful. Of course, documentaries, and my documentaries in particular, always use storytelling and character portrayals and character developments, but there is a limit to how much they can do because of the nature of the format. Whereas, if you are doing a feature film, you're basically starting from scratch and you have a lot more control over which kind of journey you're taking your audience on. I think the most powerful version of that is when you have a real story but you start writing it from scratch. With documentaries you won't be there every single moment, but with a fictional film you can recreate them. I think that has the most powerful effect on people's ability to re-experience something and "live" through it.

The Battle of Algiers was an incredible film because it exposed a story in such a real and visceral way, which allows you to experience it and then realize the film is so ambiguous about everything. It treats nobody as just the hero or just the devil. There are so many beautiful scenes that I think open a space in our minds to be able to hold complex ideas about revolution and about struggle and about injustice. That's key for us today, because we're more and more simplifying things that are so complex. We do have the ability to hold complex views of things but our media is not helping us do that. If the stories we're being told are constantly simplistic and one-sided, our brain is going to become simplistic and one-sided, because that's how it works. My goal in my work is to expand that so we can start re-developing this innate ability we have as human beings to hold complexity.

Is it possible ever to say whether nonviolent movements like in Budrus are successful?

There's no question that from the point of view of the villagers of Budrus, they succeeded in preventing the destruction of their village. But they're still living under occupation, so it's not the end of the story by any means. They had one success that was incredibly meaningful to their day-to-day life, which is the fact that they get to keep their land. But in terms of their long term safety, ability to have independence, and political freedom, they have none of that. For them the struggle is as big as it was before.

I don't think we ever achieve victory in the big "V" sense. I think we tend to decide to wrap things up at some point, like the civil rights movement. All right, the civil rights movement won but there are still a lot of battles that African Americans need to wage in this country. They're nowhere close to closing that one. It's almost like a film. You never actually finish a film. You just abandon it at one point. I think struggles for social justice are very similar to that. You work really hard and then at some point each individual decides, "OK, I've done what I can do here, and now it's the time for someone else to pick up where I left off, or for the next generation to pick it up." I don't think it's ever about achieving full victory, I think it's about achieving small successes.

PETER DAVIS

Peter Davis made *Hearts and Minds*, his Academy Award–winning documentary about America's involvement in the Vietnam War, in 1974. The film is in a style Davis describes as "adversarial," and contains candid interviews with veteran and antiwar activist Bobby Muller, former U.S. Army Chief of Staff, General William Westmoreland, and other Vietnamese and American citizens at the center of the conflict. A lot of people are still angry about it, but one gets the sense that Davis doesn't yield to anger.

Prior to *Hearts and Minds*, Davis directed documentaries for CBS News about all manner of social ills and the rebellions they inspired. His nonfiction writings include *Where is Nicaragua?* about Reagan-era policy and its impacts on Central America, and *If You Came This Way: A Journey Through the Lives of the Underclass*. In 2003, he covered the war in Iraq for *The Nation*.

Tell me about the role of documentation in times of social upheaval.

The role for me of a documentarian is to observe—take down if you're writing or film if you're filming—as accurately as possible what is going on, and then put it together in such a way that you are not hammering your potential readers or viewers, but are nonetheless interpreting the events you have either been smart enough or lucky enough to be present for. Specifically, I have never been a fan of advocacy journalism. People should write all the editorials they want to write. Most of the time that's preaching to the choir. But adversarial journalism will not try to tell you how to feel and will give you an experience rather than an explanation. I always interpret that as my job if I'm doing anything that has to do with viewers or with readers, to be their loyal adversary.

How did the attitude of Hearts and Minds *compare with the attitude of society at the time of the film's release?*

At the time *Hearts and Minds* was released, the war was winding down but there was still a great deal of controversy about it. It had been decided in the election of 1968 that the war had to end, but it wasn't ending. Nixon was elected because the people felt he had a better plan. I remember a great correspondent at CBS News named Mike Wallace—he's still living, he's about ninety or something—who said to me, "It really doesn't matter who wins this election because the war will be over in six months." Well, that wasn't a stupid opinion on his part, but not only was the war not over in six months; it wasn't over in six years.

The controversy, by the time *Hearts and Minds* came out at the very end of 1974, was over what should have been done rather than whether the war should end. People felt the left had not supported the war or else we would have won it.

So the studio that paid for *Hearts and Minds* refused to release it, not because they didn't want to lose money—they knew they'd lose a little bit of money anyway on a documentary—but because they thought that the conservative movement would say, "Hey, let's boycott the films of Columbia Pictures." Warner Brothers was run by a completely different kind of person.

There was one instance that I know about of people from the American Legion, which is a veterans' organization, generally a very conservative one, trashing the theater that played the film. Essentially, nothing else happened except that not many people went to it. But *Hearts and Minds'* shelf life, I guess, is due to the fact that a lot of people feel it has something to say about our place in the world. The film didn't "answer," so much, but I wanted it to address itself to three questions: Why did we go to Vietnam? What was it that we did there? And what did the doing in turn do to us? People seemed, not because of my film, to have learned the lesson that we don't need to go across the world and fight somebody who is no threat to us just because we disagree with their government. But then 9/11 was like a blow on our heads causing amnesia.

Do you see American society as engaged with its humanity?

Probably, but not consciously. The left is engaged with the humanity that it would like to see in America. I think the right is engaged, but I don't think the left thinks of it that way. The right is engaged with American humanity in saying we just do not want the government in our lives. Who can argue with that, really? But, unfortunately, the left, that is, the liberals, have not managed to redefine the terms of that debate, which they should because [the debate] is really not about the government interfering in lives but that's how everybody now thinks of it. It's about what experiences do we share that we want our collective manifestation (a country's collective manifestation is its government) to do? What do we want them not to do? That's the debate we should be having and we're not having it. I wish we were having a conscious debate about our humanity, but we're not. And yet I think each side is grappling with our national identity.

Why is the engagement not conscious? How does it become conscious?

I think it's not conscious probably because it almost never is and [the politicians] look alike. You like this guy because he promises this and I like that guy because . . . Although I think at certain moments, when it's far apart from one another, it becomes conscious. For instance, when Lincoln said we couldn't have slavery anymore. He was very slow to say that too. Only in the third year of his presidency did he say, "This is evil. We can't have this anymore." I think again in the 1960s we had a rather conscious debate about what kind of a society we want to have. Should everybody be equal or, because it's customary, should we keep our customs? Tradition is, after all, what has worked. But the people who were kept down said, "Well, it hasn't worked too well for us." So eventually the laws, if not the practice, did become in favor of equality. But it's rare.

Why is it so rare?

Because you're involved with issues of the moment that aren't all that fundamental to your society. Say someone says: "I believe the public employees ought to have labor unions," and someone else says, "No they shouldn't 'cause they work with the government, so labor unions for a public employee is a contradiction in terms." That's not really a debate about our identity. Or say someone says, "Higher taxes are what we need because it will level the playing field." Then someone else says, "No it won't, because it will take away from people who worked by the sweat of their brow to get their money, it's unjust." On the other hand, a friend of mine who is a tax lawyer says that tax law is a debate over what society is. It's really about social values and moral values. But most people see it in much more daily terms.

What is the process of making society's engagement with humanity more conscious?

This gets back to when you asked me how I feel about Americans. I said, worried more then scared. I'm worried because I think it may not be possible to make it conscious. The reason I come to this reluctant point of view, although it's a point of view not a conclusion, is because I hope I'm wrong, is because I don't think we've ever had a presidential candidate— maybe since Adlai Stevenson who ran against Eisenhower and lost—who tried so hard to make a political campaign about our humanity as we saw in the last election with Barack Obama. Perhaps Robert Kennedy was trying to in 1968 before he was assassinated. He tried to make his campaign about, how do we want to be? Not just what we're for, but what do we want to be?

Obama tried so hard and when he got elected there was the financial crisis, the horrible economy, the wars that he inherited. I'm not saying that some of this isn't his fault—I wish he'd had another term in the Senate to learn how the machinery works a little better—but the things he inherited made it such that he turned to people who did know the machinery: a bunch of Wall Streeters. I don't say that Larry Summers and Ben Bernanke were terrible people, but they were in the tradition of the people who had made the problem in the first place. So Obama went from being a candidate who was trying to redefine the terms of the debate to a practical president. Maybe he should have been more firm with his liberal principles, I'm not sure anything would have worked.

I also have to give the right their due. There were two other candidacies where people were talking about, in their campaigns for the presidency, the kind of society we want to be. One was Barry Goldwater and he failed, but he did the lay the groundwork for what happened later. The other was President Ronald Reagan. He won not just on a platform of saying Jimmy Carter was a bad president, but by almost making what his supporters said was a spiritual connection to our roots.

I would hope that a reconnection to basic humanity is not entirely contingent on leaders. I think the potential exists regardless.

Yes, but it's contingent on making the leadership listen, which is what Martin Luther King did and what the Occupy movement has done and what the Tea Party movement has done too. These grass-roots movements have changed the very way people look at things. But I think the aim of public life should be the same aim that psychoanalysis has, of taking those things that are unconscious and bringing them into consciousness. That's the great thing about psychoanalysis and that's the great thing about those moments in public life when people start to look again at things that they've always taken for granted.

RY COODER

I have always admired Ry Cooder's soundtrack for Wim Wenders's film *Paris, Texas* for its ability to paint a complete picture with no words. Cooder's latest direction, on *Pull Up Some Dust and Sit Down*, is a little more direct. Songs include "The Mutt Romney Blues," about the infamous incident where the presidential candidate encased his family dog on the roof of his car for a twelve-hour drive, and "No Banker Left Behind," about a quick escape route for the wealthy.

Cooder may seem angrier, but he is no less clear: Things are bad and they must be spoken about, no matter how painful it might seem.

⌘

Was there a particular moment when you realized you feel strongly about the way the world is?

I'd always heard these stories when I was a little kid. There were people my parents were friendly with who were either blacklisted or socialists or, you know, thinkers along those lines. In particular there was a family they were friendly with where the man was a blacklisted violinist—this was in the early '50s—and he ended up having to go be a camp counselor, which was a job that a lot of these professionals who were blacklisted had to do.

Musicians are always easy targets. They don't seem to have any kind of backup, there's no safety net. I don't care if you're Jascha Heifetz or the lowest hillbilly—there's a kind of vulnerability and it's easy to get rid of you. If you're a classical musician in those days you were working for powerful organizations like the Los Angeles Philharmonic, which was in turn controlled by money. Those people, they play hardball. If there was any taint on you, you were gone. So that particular man [blacklisted violinist] gave me my first guitar when I was four. I think he knew I liked music and that I'd be good at it [laughs].

76

These were classical musicians and so forth, highly cultured people—but folk music came into prominence in these intellectual circles because they felt there was a need to join with the proletariat or the working class. Pete Seeger and others. Know what I mean? You have Woody Guthrie do your soiree in your beautiful rich house. It's a fabulous idea and very realistic in Los Angeles because of the kind of democratic social landscape. Of course, as always, provided you're white. That should go without saying. But there was this desire for a kind of up and down the ladder movement.

So your connection to music and your awareness of the effect the violinist's politics had on his professional life came at the same time.

You have to understand, all I knew was Leo was having a hard time. He's a camp counselor now. They didn't tell me these things, they didn't educate me, they didn't quite sit me down like they should have. But the idea was that these people, this family, their house where I went often, not far from where we lived in Santa Monica, was a treasure trove for me. They had all the old Folkways records, Pete Seeger, the Woody Guthrie gospel songs, which included some of those Farm Security photographs. And *Pogo* books. The *Pogo* books really fascinated me because it was so interesting how the animals talked. Their little scenes depicted all of the McCarthy goings and comings.

So there was a lot of this but there was also the background talk about, of course, all that McCarthy stuff, all of the FBI investigations, all of the business about Chavez Ravine here in Los Angeles. They didn't seem to think I would understand but they were wrong because kids can understand a lot.

Kids can sometimes be more attuned to some instinctive sense of right and wrong.

But people in those days still clung to this belief that there'd be an end to class warfare and class struggle. These were educated people and they had a good grasp of history, but it didn't work out that way, did it? I mean, quite the opposite. Today we have this nightmare situation.

So growing up, I got to like populist music. You had the music that had gone on before Pete Seeger and so on, chiefly from the Depression era. Populist music really flowered then because of the issues: hobos and the train songs and the work songs and all of this, the big man against the little man and workers against the bosses. This was fantastic for music. So I got to like that stuff and learned how to play it, guitars and banjos and mandolins.

I always have thought that our music in America, vernacular music, is not the music of happy times. When the people on the street go to make up a song, they don't sing about how great everything is, they sing about how hard everything is. They sing about what they're up against, the odds they're up against, the terrible struggle of it all. And of course it's narrative, it's very visual when you hear these tunes. Woody's songs about the Dust Bowl are perfectly done. I used to think when I was younger he was exaggerating, and then I learned that he wasn't, it was eyewitness accounts in those songs, exactly as he wrote them down. What he saw, what he was able to make songs out of, was totally true. I've seen pictures of it now, photographs. It's unbelievable. Like nothing that had ever been seen.

You mentioned before how musicians and musical culture is vulnerable, and I suppose it has only become more so with time.

Oh yeah, sure. People are [vulnerable]. Cultures that people make for themselves never survive the onslaught or the penetration of market capital, or whatever you want to call that. Just can't survive it. [It's all about] the individual's own feeling, what you *feel*. Do you even know what that is? I don't know how people with their little screens are ever going to find out. I'm very worried that young people won't ever have the presence of mind or the habit of mind to even say: I wonder what *I* think. Because they've become pawns in this whole setup. But the thing I like about music, and I still like to do it, I mean . . . Sit down, take the guitar or your mandolin, whatever you have, and play—and just hear it and just feel it. If you can do that in some way that reflects almost nothing but pure energy, it's just like, OK, let me make a sound that I like. Nobody has to tell me about it, I'm not making money when I'm doing it. It's not a transaction of any kind. So that's the thing to try to preserve.

Surely, though, the act of making an album like the one that you've just made, the act of continuing to do what you do, is a hopeful act.

Well, I think so. But I have no hope. Pete Seeger recently said—and I put this in one of the songs— "I have no hope, I could be wrong." It was the first pessimistic thing he's ever said in his life. You know, he's in his nineties now and I asked a friend of mine who's close to him, "What's

Pete saying these days?" "I have no hope, I could be wrong." That's really shocking. That is so radical for Pete Seeger, the most optimistic man on the planet, the most relentlessly positive human being I ever saw in my life, almost to the point of mania, because he had this sense of mission and he has this tremendous influence over people which is totally denied, of course . . . But for him to say, "I have no hope, I could be wrong," is so shocking, and I'm with him.

At the same time if you give into this, then they've won and you've lost. With this in mind, I go and I look for ideas or things I can do and write little tunes. And if nobody hears these, I still wrote them. I sit in this chair where I am right now and jot these things down and then when I got a couple, I go with my son Joachim who plays the drums for me and we go to the home of an engineer, in his living room, we've got a few microphones set up, we just record a few of them and then work on them a little and go with the next one. So first of all it's enjoyable, as me and Joachim grew this together and he's so great at it and I have such a good time with him. And that's life as far as I'm concerned: your son and yourself, having a nice afternoon, reflecting on how this is in our lives and in his too. Needless to say, he's the one with the problem. I'm sixty-five. I'm happy to step off gracefully, like Archie Rice in *The Entertainer*. He's thirty-three. He's got to make his way somehow.

What is he thinking about at the moment?

He's thinking about how impossible it all is. In terms of records, we all wanted to do this and he grew up seeing me do it and wanting to be part of it and enjoy it and have it in his life. He saw it as a good life. Very, very interesting way to live. You support yourself as you can. I always taught him, all you need in life is a tank of gas a week—you use up too much gas, you're spending too much time in your car and that's not good—you need a roof over your head, no bars on the windows, which would be nice, and, I don't know, a broiled chicken sandwich three times a week. If you can get that, you're ahead of the curve, you're ahead of 99 percent of the people in the world. And you get to play your instrument and if you play well and do beautiful things then people will love you, or at least enjoy it, and you get to keep doing it. I don't know what more you can ask for. So he likes to do it and he does it well and he creates good things. There was a time he said, "Nobody is home anymore." I said, "Right, they've all left the building." He said, "How are we supposed to operate?" I said, "I don't know how we're all supposed to operate."

I get the sense that having the songs out there in public is great, but it's not necessarily your focus. It's not an outcome-based practice.

Well, with these political songs, to get the word out is important right now because what the song can do is create another context for looking at something. If a song says things, for instance, you can say the Koch Brothers made their deal with Satan, well, I *get* that. Where else did this power come from? That is what a song can say. The style of the music becomes part of the story and informs it and then people listen and say, "Oh, I see what the metaphor is." You couldn't say that in a book, you certainly couldn't stand at a podium at some school giving this lecture. People would think you'd lost your mind. But then in a song you get it, because the song tells you in a couple of different ways.

Obama pacing up and down the Oval Office at three in the morning: That makes a really good song, the terror and the loneliness of it. How do you say that? How do you describe that? Well, by the sound of the song. So this is where the stuff I've listened to all my life. I understand it; I know how to use it. It's a technique. And so of course I want people to get this message if they can. At the same time I also know that nobody but nobody is buying CDs anymore, so what am I going to do with these tunes? I haven't figured out if I'm going to just give them away on some website. Whoever's got the biggest listenership or readership, *you* take them. The commerce idea is gone.

You have songs on the album that are full of frustration and anger and then you have songs that really poke fun at the current political climate. Do you think there is an equal place for both?

Well, what happens with these things is I wait for an idea to arrive, because I don't know where the next one is coming from. I get an idea or I read something or I hear somebody talking about something. Some are going to be funny and some are going to be not funny like the one about the guy whose daughter says she just joined the Army. That's a horrible tragedy. We all know about how in Los Angeles the Army recruiters go to poor schools in poor neighborhoods and they target, of course, African American kids and Mexican kids. It's one of the most nefarious and odious things. We're supposed to be protecting the lives of young people? What a joke. You're throwing them to the wolves, getting them killed. It's a scandal; I can barely talk about it. I happen to know because I have friends who are on the front lines just trying to stop it. They get abuse, these two people I know. I said, "What are you going to do today?" They said, "Well, we're going downtown to leaflet the school, probably to get kicked and spit on." I said, "Jesus Christ."

I went home so horrified at the story and about how the school district could be in on this. I just couldn't stand it. They said, "No, don't get mad, get even. Write a tune." So, then, that's what came, the song about the schools. I keep my ears open, I'm just going to keep doing these things I guess. If you're listening to what people are saying, you have to think it out. You can't just go blundering around. You have to analyze the stuff so that you get to the core of it. Then you can do your three-minute song.

You said that you're in solidarity with that idea of not having hope, but you could be wrong. Do you feel like you will be proved wrong in time?

What I love in this world is being destroyed—that's the natural world, nature in California, if you want to be specific. The country is in the hands of C and D students who only know aggression and greed, and the record business has been rigged. The next thing to go will be books. I'll cut my wrists in the bathtub before I ever touch a Kindle. You can't read a newspaper anymore without throwing up. But not to complain, I'm not complaining. I remember things very vividly and it's all like yesterday to me, and all these things I miss so much—a quality of everyday life—is disappearing, the tempo of it, the texture of it. It's not something I feel isolated in my feeling for. If you read your Orwell, he pretty much called it. I'm amazed how [*1984*] captured the whole essence of the thing. But as individuals . . . we have friends who are artists who get up every day and do their work regardless. They work twelve, fourteen hours a day in their art studios and make beautiful art and that's an affirmation and a constant discipline and a constant belief. I don't know what else you want out of life. I try to do it too, I think that's what life is really all about.

ROBERT FULLER

Robert Fuller is the former president of Oberlin College and the author of three books—*Somebodies and Nobodies: Overcoming the Abuse of Rank*, *All Rise: Somebodies, Nobodies and the Politics of Dignity* and *Dignity for All: How to Create a World Without Rankism*—on what he has termed "rankism." This term, in part derived from Fuller's desire to galvanize society around a common enemy and in part from a sound understanding of human hierarchical tendency, means "abusive, discriminatory, or exploitative behavior towards people because of their rank in a particular hierarchy."

Fuller has a PhD in physics from Princeton University and is the co-author of another book about precarious relationships: *Mathematics of Classical and Quantum Physics* with Frederick Byron Jr.

❦

How did you come from studying physics to be concerned with human behavior?

I think we take on certain questions in childhood, contradictions that are right in our face as five-year-olds and ten-year-olds. These can trump what it is you set out to do as a professional, and that's what happened to me. As the civil rights movement and the women's movement took off in the United States, I felt a resonance with both of those. I noticed I was spending my time tracking that, not solving equations any longer, although for a while I was certain I had to be a physicist like my father. But as it turned out, my mother's passions were the ones that had taken hold and trumped my desire to understand how the world works; I wanted more to understand why the world was so unkind.

In the world of professional physics, I experienced a lot of unkindness and indignity. They're a cutthroat bunch of guys who think that they're the smartest guys in the world. You can make a case that they're awfully clever and that the consequences of their work are incredibly important. My own dad co-invented the solar cell, for example, a relatively benign invention. The father of my best friend in college co-invented the atom bomb. The scientists in the Manhattan Project feared that Hitler was going to make one so they did it first. I mowed the lawn of the guy who co-invented the transistor. I got to see him as a person, not as a Nobel Prize winner.

Early on I was very affected by affronts to dignity and I remember them well. I remember in second grade, probably the signature incident in my life's work, seeing a classmate of mine named Arlene sent to the hall for the whole day because she had dirty fingernails. I put this story in *Somebodies and Nobodies*. As we went to recess, we filed past Arlene, who was standing near the water fountain slumped against the wall avoiding our eyes, and I thought, "That could be me." But that never would have been me. Know why? Because my mom would have gone after the teacher. My mom was a force in that town. My dad was famous. They weren't going to mess with me. I didn't realize that at the time, but I did feel vaguely protected. But Arlene's parents were dirt farmers, so she was vulnerable.

There were no blacks because my town was so bigoted that it didn't even allow blacks to live in it, let alone attend the school. There were very educated people within a few miles of Chatham [New Jersey] because of Bell Labs, but Chatham itself had these not-atypical real estate agreements that precluded any person of color buying a home in the town. That kind of thing dawned on me, because our basketball team would play other nearby towns and there'd be black people on those teams, but not on my team. Later, I realized that I was a beneficiary of the racist real estate policy, because I probably wouldn't have made the team if I'd had to compete with blacks.

Did you ever have conversations with your parents about what you were observing?

Not until college, which I went to young. I skipped a few grades and found myself in college at fifteen. Within months I realized, oh my God, the America I'd grown up believing in is actually unjust. By Thanksgiving of my first year in college, we were having pitched battles over the turkey and I was strident and cocksure of my new set of values and didn't really give my parents their due—because I saw them as supporting the political status quo. Then I get to graduate school, and there were all these guys who thought they were the smartest guys in the world and the game they played was called "one-upmanship." Everything is "trivial," that's the way they talked. That was the first time I think I was ever treated with indignity myself.

Why do you think you were able to transcend the experience of being ridiculed, as opposed to letting it define your own behavior?

What it was is that I had a secure upbringing and a privileged education. It gave me strength. I knew that these guys were making fun of me, but I could easily see that there were groups of other people getting a far worse deal. It's a stretch for me even to recall the indignities I suffered growing up, they were few and far between. I could be arrogant myself on occasion, and of course you end up committing certain behaviors you are ashamed of later just because it's in the air.

I shared a small office with my world famous professor when he took a sabbatical to Berkeley. That made for a priceless mentorship. You get to see how he handles his own mistakes; you get to see how he talks to his wife, how he treats his kids, how he talks to his secretary. He got the National Medal of Science from the White House and he took with him, when he got it, his black gardener. He was very unusual.

Do you believe in human nature?

I think human nature is malleable. When I grew up sexism was called human nature. So I am very skeptical of [the idea of] something indelibly written in our genes. I think we are a work in progress and everything that we take for granted as human nature won't look like that 100 years from now. My main evidence for this is the de-legitimization of six 'isms' in my lifetime, starting with anti-Semitism, then racism, sexism, heterosexualism—or homophobia—ageism, and colonialism. All those isms were explained as part of human nature, and even people as enlightened as George Washington and Abraham Lincoln felt it was human nature that people of dark skin were mentally inferior. What is it we take for granted now? My guess is it's going to be something as fundamental as selfhood. I think we're in the process of deconstructing selfhood. The little ghost we feel might be inside us—"myself"—is really a fiction, agreed upon, and more like computer code than it is like a willful little person.

I would put it to you that something fundamental to all humans—and perhaps, in that sense, "human nature"—is our equal ability to be humiliated and to humiliate.

I have caught myself doing that after having it done to me. It's the old eye for eye, tooth for tooth morality. We do to others what's done to us until we catch ourselves doing it. I've now caught myself and stopped meeting every indignity with one of my own.

Do you think the capacity remains but what's changed is your awareness?

Within myself I'll always have the old code, the old programs, the old racist slurs, but I don't emit them. My kids don't even have them in their programming and my grandkids are multiracial. There's a sense in which there's an attenuation of this stuff, which you might be thinking is human nature. I don't even think the tit-for-tat of meeting one indignity with another is human nature. I think we can get over that and immediately sense that if we do it, we will be perpetuating the rankism in the world and it might sooner or later come back to hit us. We learn to nip certain sequences of behavior in the bud.

What is the importance of self-awareness to correcting behaviors we might otherwise assume to be "human nature?"

Huge. It's the "witness function" in this wonderful "machine." We have enough spare capacity to devote part of our mind to watching the rest of the machine. I've been asking people lately about how aware they are of their own witness; in other words, do they have a witness to the witness? And they do! Even little kids do. I remember I asked my dad this when he was ninety, and he said, "Yes, I do. In fact, it's the same part of me that was looking through the holes in the fence when I was five years old." He felt like that part of him that was watching himself non-judgmentally at five was still watching at ninety. The witness is your best friend and can bring about a change of course in the rest of the machinery, although that takes heightened awareness and practice and repetition.

In a way, a movement could be said to be the same thing manifested en masse. The witness is internal consciousness-raising, a movement is external.

The internal awareness writ large, it's a wonderful idea. Iris Murdoch said, "Man is a creature who makes pictures of himself and then comes to resemble the picture." That's the idea of memes being imitated and spreading and rippling right across the world. Occupy Wall Street is the consciousness that many of us have had, writ large, beginning to manifest in the world. That's why some are so eager to denounce it and shame it, just as people were with the first awareness of feminist values.

Once people stand up for dignity it's not long until they're marching for justice, and that's the transition we're seeing in Occupy Wall Street. Dignity is the core value, the animating force, in the Arab Spring, in Occupy Wall Street, in the streets of Moscow and Wukan. A movement needs to know not only what it's for, but what it's against. That's why I introduced the notion of rankism, as the "ism" that the dignity movement opposes.

The cause of indignity is not that someone outranks you. The cause of indignity is when someone who outranks you abuses the power inherent in their rank to put you down. It's a precise thing. That's the trouble with egalitarianism, which suggests equality of rank. No! We love people of higher rank if they treat us with dignity. We admire them, we want to learn from them. If they've earned their rank and they exemplify kindness and dignity. The best parents, the best teachers, are people like that, but when they use the powers of their rank to demean us, then the war is on.

Is it possible to have a society where there is an equal level of dignity but not of rank?

Yes. Social ranks are all specious. One after another, they have been disallowed. They were the truisms that turned out to be falsities that I grew up with. Social ranks such as white outranks black, straight outranks gay, are no longer considered credible or legitimate. But rank in an organization is a useful tool for getting things done. However, the notion of rank is going to change tremendously: Ranks are going to be temporary, and we will make hierarchies in the name of getting something done efficiently, but then we'll go on to another task with a new hierarchy. So rank becomes just a tool of organization.

You cannot absolutely ensure against abuse of power but it becomes less likely when the person in power realizes that he will not have that rank after a certain time. There really are people who are more gifted leaders than other people and they are always people who honor the dignity of their subordinates. The idea that you can beat people into greater creativity and productivity is an idea that's wrong. People are rapidly coming to see this now and so all those nineteenth-century practices in education and business are being jettisoned.

When you're in the middle of a movement and it has not reached the point where you can categorically say it's a success, how do you reconcile the undesirable parts of it?

Here's an example: the gay movement. I knew upfront before it had even shown its face, that it would win that it was right. As a young man, I had a personal aversion to homosexuality but it was clear to me from the start that it was an issue of human dignity. Then the movement manifests and lo and behold there are guys parading around in leather codpieces, but I stick with the cause because I know that it's about human dignity. So there's your answer. You keep your eye on the star: Is this movement expanding the circle of human dignity? If it is, you stick with the excesses. You overlook them. I was a college president in 1970 and a few students came in to see me in my office about holding a gay dance on campus. Believe me, this was not a welcome idea in 1970 but I could deduce that it had to happen and was ready to fight the board of trustees and resign if they didn't allow it. The students held the dance, my wife and I went. You have to show your support for the principle of equal dignity for all.

Is it dignity or humiliation that mobilizes people?

It's the same as in the civil rights movement: it's the indignity they're suffering that finally galvanizes victims to resist. Then there are two ways of resisting: One is to do back to your tormentors what they're doing to you—John Brown tried it, and he was caught and executed. And there's the Gandhi and Martin Luther King Jr. way of doing it: not doing back what was done to you but raising the cost to the perpetrators by disrupting society so much that people say, "Oh well, we might as well let them in because if we don't everything is going to come to a standstill." You have to make the price very high, but, in the end, these techniques of disruption are more powerful than techniques of destruction. Victims can just sit on their hands—a general strike. And that would be my dream for OWS: if they could organize things up to the point where they say, "We ain't moving. You're going to change it or we ain't moving." But organizing something like that is incredibly complicated. The real heroes of the world are the community organizers who manage to gather large numbers of people, each one with a small amount of power, but you multiply that small number by a lot of folks and it finally trumps the power of the self-serving elite. That's what we may be seeing now. The idea of dignity is to give people something that they're willing to stand up for in the abstract, and then they undertake to overcome the particular injustices that afflict them.

What do you see when you look at contemporary American society?

In the '60s, I knew that America was in a life and death struggle but I was really convinced that the dignitarian forces were going to win. But now we're up against a much deeper malady: the abuse of power, as vested in rank. I doubt that Americans will be the first to get their heads around this, somehow.

What's remarkable about OWS is that it's the first effort to raise this fundamental issue, but I don't know if rankism is a sufficiently good rallying cry. It hasn't worked so far. The connection between indignity and rankism has yet to be made. I don't think OWS has an analysis yet of their movement and I do think they need one if it's going to continue to grow and finally bring some justice.

I haven't given up hope but it's going to be by a very close shave that this country makes it if we do. [There's a] failure to understand that we don't do anything by ourselves, that selfhood is a co-creation. Not only do we not build a business by ourselves, we don't even exist by ourselves. Most people are still acting as if, "I'm autonomous, I created myself, I don't need you." Well, we do need others, because if you're put in solitary confinement your whole identity disintegrates. You have to be talking; you have to be exchanging memes all the time. We're mutually dependent even for the existence of our "selves." I'm not religious but the world's religions all have a lot to say about this issue. And a lot of the more inclusive politics follows from according equal dignity to all. I think it's the only way forward for humankind. There could be gigantic setbacks like climate change and nuclear war, but we could possibly sneak through into a dignitarian world. We could fail in our first try, but we are destined to become one human family in the long run.

FRANCES FOX PIVEN

In May 1968, *Life* magazine published a picture of Frances Fox Piven, then a professor of social work at Columbia, and her daughter. They are climbing into a building, occupied by student participants in the 1968 strike at Columbia, assisted by the activist Tom Hayden. This is one of the first pictures to appear when you search Piven's name online and it remains a powerful image of her commitment to radical action.

Piven is the co-author, with Richard Cloward, of the Cloward-Piven Strategy, a call to overload the American public welfare system to incite default, "a strategy for forcing political change through orchestrated crisis." She is the author of *Challenging Authority: How Ordinary People Change America* and *Who's Afraid of Frances Fox Piven? The Essential Writings of the Professor Glenn Beck Loves to Hate.*

* * *

You wrote an article called "A Proud, Angry Poor" for The Nation *about how shame makes protest less likely. What are the political consequences of loss of dignity?*

The loss of dignity is a little bit different than not having any dignity in the first place. The loss of dignity suggests a process of active degradation of a person or a group. The political consequences of that process can't be stated definitively because it depends on a lot of other things. Certainly, if you take for granted that the main thing that is happening is that the society is stripping people of standing, and that people are not resistant, not reacting, not reclaiming their dignity, then the consequence will be to make it much less likely if not impossible for people to be active participants in critical protests.

But those conditions almost never hold because people fight back. They may not be able to do it right in that moment or even in that year, but people have ways of reclaiming dignity. They have a yearning to reclaim their dignity and they have the capacity to reclaim their dignity and they do it by redefining the reasons for their circumstances. This society or the dominating group that is degrading them says that the reasons for their condition, such as poverty, are within them. But people get together and have different ideas. The attribution of blame and the awarding of status in our culture has so many complicated facets. There are a lot of resources in our society and European society—I'm not sure if that's true everywhere—for people to fight back and reassert their rights and their entitlement to participate in a more democratic process of attributing blame and attributing of valued resources.

You have said that you, and people you know, are not talking or thinking in terms of "revolution." Why is this?

I think I speak for myself and a lot of people like me, including younger people in the protest movements, when I say that there are two reasons: one is that we don't have a history of revolutions of which we are proud, which we think solve the problems that animated some of the revolutionary forces. So there isn't an experience in successful humanitarian, democratic, socialist terms of revolution. The other reason is, not only do we not have the history, we don't have theories in which we can have any confidence on how to transform a society. That's what makes me a reformist, but I think it takes an incredible amount of mobilization from the bottom to get any reform. If you were able to generate the kind of instability in the United States or in the West that we associate with revolution, I don't know what would happen. That's why I think people shy away from revolution. It can create great chaos and uncertainty, especially at a time in history when States are such powerful military forces, when ruling classes seem to be out of control and not particularly rooted in their native countries.

Is radical change the only worthwhile change?

No. I work for small changes and I always have. I've worked for fourteen years to get a more open voter registration system and in most places it wasn't even implemented, so no.

How do you maintain your conviction?

I test and reevaluate my convictions continually and I also think that I have a wonderful life. There's no self-sacrifice in my political vocation and I don't particularly regard myself as having been hurt or martyred, I'm very fortunate and I enjoy what I do and I have good comrades. The development of history constantly reaffirms my ideas, so my ideas do change but not in their broadest compass.

Do you consider yourself a hopeful person?

I'm hopeful in temperament but I don't think my intellectual analysis is especially hopeful. I see our future as very troubled and very uncertain, but I'm hopeful about particular efforts that I'm involved in nevertheless. I just think you have to keep the satisfaction that you get out of trying to do things, you have to give that full weight, and at the same time you have to be serious and intelligent about the forces that work in the world, which you're trying to offset or change. I'm proud of what I do.

That element of pride and dignity is important in mobilizing people. Has there been a particular time when you've seen that?

I think you can see it almost any time but in the 1960s I worked a lot with welfare recipients who mobilized in the welfare rights movement. The movement subsided in the early 1970s but there are a lot of particular groups that either remained or new groups that formed—vital groups of women, poor women, most of them minorities who were asserting their rights and trying to change policies and so forth. They're always there, in a sense, it's just that far fewer people are engaged with them. What they do, even when everything is against them, is they keep alive the possibility of an alternative interpretation of why we are poor and they keep alive an example of fighting back, so that it's not restricted to particular periods of the 1930s or the 1960s. It's been there all along but it engages more people at times, like right now I think a movement is growing in the United States. Under some conditions it's very difficult to make that kind of self-assertion. People do have that capacity, but the capacity to claim dignity can also be crushed by social conditions, social influences. So there's nothing inevitable about rebellion.

What are the conditions that produce rebellion?

I think that hardship is a precondition, but it's far and away from being the main condition. People have to be able to see that the conditions under which they live are unjust. And that depends a lot on the culture they inherit and contradictions in that culture. For example, right now in the United States people are losing their homes because they were foolish and they took out mortgages and used those mortgages as an ATM machine. You could blame yourself, you know, if you had done that over a period. You didn't read the fine print in the mortgage. But who can read the fine print? Nobody. You signed there on that dotted line and you screwed everything up.

But then, when stories abound about finagling of middle men in the mortgage industry and the banks and Freddie Mac, well, it's not my fault anymore. It happened to millions of people because [the banks] are shysters. [People] were in no position to say that those guys were cheating [the public] because they're high status people. But when [the banks] were discredited by the press, that was a condition which made it easier for people to assert their own interpretation of what they were owed in terms of respect and goods and money.

Sometimes the form it takes is that dominant groups, elites, don't want to abide any longer by traditional norms, even the norms which benefitted them, because the world is changing, markets are changing; they become more greedy, more ambitious. When elites violate traditional norms, including norms that privilege elites, they become also susceptible to this kind of discrediting, historically.

This has been a remarkable period for discrediting and also for material change. People lost their homes. They lost about 20 percent of their earnings. A lot of them are unemployed. Young people coming out of school have $25,000, $50,000 worth of debt and they can't get a job. So people lost a lot, but that's not enough. They also need to be able to figure out that it wasn't their fault.

Also in that article for The Nation, *you wrote, "A proud and angry poor could help to remake America." What do you see when you look at American society?*

I think America is becoming inefficient and increasingly corrupt. All sorts of things don't work. My home phone, sometimes I can't get a dial tone; I'd say half the time I can't use it. There's a critique of American capitalism because it generates a lot of inequality. I'm saying it generates a lot of inefficiency. And you know, you try to get something fixed, you place a call to the service number, somebody picks up the phone in Bangladesh. What are the odds of it getting fixed? They're not great.

There are all sorts of people in the United States. It's a very diverse country and it always has been. But I think there are a substantial number of Americans who are reacting to big societal change in the most destructive way possible. They become very reactionary; they're lashing out at foreigners, black people. They imagine that they can return to an idyllic past, which never existed. These are people who are not actually hurting. These are people who are just distressed, anxious that there are changes in the country. Then there are a lot of people who are poor, for the first time in a long time. We have a poverty line that calls "poor" anything below $22,000 a year for a family of four. A family of four on $22,000 is really poor. And that's a lower poverty line than other relatively affluent countries use. If you use a more reasonable poverty line, probably about 100 million people are poor in the United States. That means they're insecure, that they can't get the kids the things the kids have to have so that other kids don't make fun of them. And we're a big war-maker. And we contribute mightily to climate change, which may doom us all. I mean, there are a lot of things wrong.

Is the challenge to still be able to see—not even to create, but to see—the possibility for an alternative?

Yes, and we work at it in multiple ways all the time. I personally believe that it takes a lot of upheaval and a lot of trouble from the bottom to shake those in authority into either conceding space for change or making the changes themselves. And I don't have a big blueprint for how to solve all these problems. I think we just try. That's the point, because it makes life possible. In that sense, it's the point.

You have said before that the assumption is that people shape movements, but in fact movements can equally shape people.

I do think experience in movements can transform people. But I think movement power is the result of the trouble movements make, and that trouble I have variously called disruption. Movements can shut things down. They can tap the power that is inherent in the fact that we all play a role in a series of institutions. That's what social life is. It's a complex system of collaboration, and we can all refuse to play our roles. We can refuse to go to school; we can refuse to go to work; we can refuse to be the nannies for the upper class women who go to work on Wall Street. We can refuse.

Is there an element of symbolic power in movements, as well as practical power?

I think there's a relationship between a kind of symbolic defiance and actual defiance. Movements are very good makers of symbols and very good communicators of symbols because they obviously don't have a billion dollars for an ad campaign, yet if they can create a symbol that has resonance with people, like "We are the 99 percent," or "Occupy Wall Street"—if they can fashion their symbols, the movement repertoire is how to project those symbols. We have our big banners and our marches and our demos. Occupation was even better, because a demonstration is over in three hours but occupation isn't. But then, that's still the communicative aspect of movements. Movements also, by projecting a vision of change and strength from the bottom, can encourage people not to play the conforming role that they ordinarily play. And if people don't play that role, things stop. It's when things stop that those in authority have to do something.

COLTER JACOBSEN

Colter Jacobsen is an artist. Recently, I saw his work *Claire de Lune*, two graphite drawings of the moon on yellowed record sleeves, as part of SFMOMA's 2010 SECA Art Award. Jacobsen's work often features sets of images that are *near* identical, which gives the viewer a familiar feeling that what was promised has not been delivered. Within that break in expectation, something imperfect but inarguably beautiful takes its place.

Jacobsen's work has been exhibited at White Columns and at the Vilnuis Trienniel in Lithuania. He is represented by Jack Hanley Gallery and Corvi-Mora (UK).

* * *

You have said that your understanding of politics is peripheral and through practical means.

Global politics is hard to comprehend. What do I really know about the Arab Spring? I've just picked things up from the news or from friends and it's in pieces. It's hard to say, do I really know what's going on over there? And then to think, well, do I even understand what's happening right here? It seems so overwhelming. So, yes, for me useful politics is politics I can understand. The immediate politics of economic exchanges, like buying something when I know where it came from or the people who made it. Or selling one of my books: I get the social interaction and I know exactly whom the book is going to. Our times demand something more from people who aren't necessarily out on the street or on the front lines with the police. You can't help but have a relationship to politics and the politics of economy.

I think a lot of things I'm doing could be seen as radical, perhaps political: something as simple as writing a song as a gay man about my love for another man. Politics in that way is very much about your everyday relationships. You go out and move in space and it can be political. What you buy, all this, it's inevitably charged.

There's a class that I've been a part of lately. We meet every Thursday but I'm not paying to be a part of it and the teacher is giving his knowledge freely. It's Japanese woodwork and joinery. We've been meeting at a mill in West Oakland for longer than a year to work on this house. It's modular, and will eventually be put up on my boyfriend's land. The idea has changed a lot but we're thinking of it almost as a possible residency or free school. I'm not really sure of the overall structure of the building. Parts of it are still very abstract but yet we're building it piece by piece. At the same time we are thinking about how the building will function as a residency or school.

For a while the conversation turned into the possibility of buying land together. It just woke us up to how much more those involved would invest in the idea of a school if they owned part of the property it was on. A lot came out: Everyone had their own interest in what they wanted land for and what ownership means, too. It also woke me up to the conflict of a new thing. If we do this, if we all go in on this together, there will continue to be costs and ramifications and we will have to deal with those.

And, of course, working together always reveals strange conflicting ideas of how best to operate in a group.

I went to an event at the Berkeley Art Museum recently on Friday night as part of their L@TE Program. It was in a reading room and there were all these books donated by three poetry presses. It's supposed to be "an experiment in an economy of literary exchange," where you exchange one book for another book. A poet, Tom Comitta, did something he calls a "Guerilla Opera." I was expecting your typical poetry reading, sitting down and listening to some poems by Tom. Instead, he proposed to the audience that we all join him for forty minutes in reading or singing from the books in the room. And so he counted down—and then everyone just started as if they'd been waiting their whole life to read loudly from text, all at the same time. It was crazy.

The thought came to me that this was similar to the Occupy Oakland movement: this kind of chaos or openness to really speak your mind and have no central message, which may be the central message. Then little things started to happen within that: two people would get together and read from the same book, rhythms would start, like some hippie drum circle jam or something, pounding on the bookshelves. Some people weren't paying attention to the books at all and were just screaming or yelling. It was pretty chaotic, though these small, organized groups, micro-associations, would develop within the chaos. Tom had to really yell to get people to stop. The big difference between this and the Occupy movement was that we had permission to be in the space.

What do you think "radical" could mean that is different to how we understand it now? What do you think constitutes radical action?

I don't know. So much has been done in the past. What would be radical to me is turning off the computer—now—and keeping it off for a long time. At the same time I do think you can really build your own reality: to want to wake up to something new that you want, I guess.

What made you want to participate in building the house?

I think being social with people is my first reason. And really admiring the people who are involved and also just a curiosity, knowing that I put something together, something so basic and fundamental as building a house. I never thought I'd be doing something like this. I'm not a wood worker. It's the same with bee-keeping. I never thought I'd be a beekeeper but my boyfriend suggested we get a hive and now I love watching bees up close and seeing the larvae grow.

As I'm telling you this I'm listening to myself and I'm noticing that it's like, I didn't initiate all this. It took a lot of people to create it and I couldn't say whose idea was what or when the idea of a school came up. Having a conversation is just relaying information, trying to learn, to get closer to something collectively.

A friend was describing this term used by the artist and poet Cecilia Vicuña in a talk about her film, *Kon Kon*: "a unity of dissonances"—which I thought was beautiful. She was talking about an old instrument, a stone flute. She drew the inside of the flute and it was two connected shafts, one large and one narrow, and those two shafts cause the dissonance and the sound. It made me think of the need to accept that. Maybe that's the key.

Many people would say the same of how to stick it out in a movement.

It's complicated though. Part of the Occupy group seems to be comprised of people who call themselves anarchists. And it's often these so-called anarchists that get the most media attention. There was something in the news about the last Oakland [demonstration] where somebody destroyed a children's exhibit, a miniature model of the Oakland city hall or something, which is kind of an amazing symbol unto itself. But one person's action isn't necessarily shared by a larger group and it's these kinds of things that are generally used in media to portray the Occupy movement negatively.

There are people who want to take the nonviolent approach but they're infiltrated by a smaller group [who don't] and then defined by that. To try to accept that is hard. I understand their anger because they feel the world that's built around them is out of their hands and that's their only way to assert their power, but it's a hard thing to reconcile.

Even at the reading I was describing, some people were just screaming. It's interesting that that's what they chose to do with the time. Something inspired them to scream. At that moment, screaming was not my sentiment. And actually, I found one person to be particularly annoying and loud, right in my ear, but then I realized I could walk away from it so I did. I found people I could read and sing along with and that was empowering. At one point I was reading parts from a play with a stranger. In the play, there was this surreal exchange about ass pounding and fisting! What a way to meet somebody!

It's easy to say this because Occupy has happened and is still happening, but people must have really needed to create a space where they could have that freedom to express what they felt like they could not express otherwise.

It's sort of like the people were almost squeezed into doing it. That's the image I have: the pressures of the powers that be, which keep pushing the people into [reacting]. It's funny because we're really lucky too. We're such lucky people to live in America and to have these freedoms and be able to voice our opinion on the street and not immediately be shut up. Sure, there are plenty of problems with America but, you know, we're not a third world country, yet we still feel squeezed despite all that. The pressure is coming down and people are starting to notice.

Maybe what put people over the edge was just an attempt to add a fee on the ATM cards for banks or something—which actually is huge—or one last thing where people feel like they're being kicked in the gut by the bank after they've watched the government give the bank a huge chunk of money that came from people's pockets.

Do you think that Occupy suggests that people believe in an alternative?

I think that's what it must mean, of course. I think that's always present and it's always the main urge. It could be quite a small [motivator] or it could be huge, like for a gay person to just want to be accepted and to create a world that is totally tolerant of their way of life. I'm sure each person has their own reason and their own way that they see that things could be better. I want to believe in an alternative, I just don't have the alternative. I try to build it every day. I am skeptical of utopia, I don't think there's necessarily a perfect system out there, but I think democracy is pretty good for what it is. There are so many important aspects within democracy. Even though there are some problems, it's what we have and we should try to make it work.

Perhaps the emphasis should not be on a re-systematizing of the country, which I cannot help but feel is completely abstract, but on practicalities, like the way systems work in our own lives and how we can change those.

I remember when I was going to school at the San Francisco Art Institute, I was very focused on the May '68 [uprising] in Paris and around the world, all the student demonstrations. I think I was most drawn to the poetry of it. I wrote up a couple of self-directed courses centering on the events at the Sorbonne and studying essays and films that came from the demonstrations. My advisor at the time was Bill Berkson and I recall at one point, after showing him a mess of a draft that had all kinds of notes, he turned to me and asked, "What is your '68?" It really caught me off guard. And I decided to respond by interviewing my parents since I wasn't around in 1968. What I found was something probably more informative than studying a demonstration across the ocean years ago. In looking back I wonder if I was just taken with the romanticism and wild action that was '68. It was very enlightening for some reason to hear from my parents about their ambivalence to the political unrest of the '60s, how they were an odd kind of conservative, back-to-the-land type. They wanted to be self-sufficient, grow a garden, raise animals, and live in the country. Instead they moved to the suburbs, converted to Mormonism, and had a huge family while my father worked a computer job that he never liked. What made him give up his dream? In this context, what is radical? Being radical is always contextual. It always needs to be seen in relation to something else. For me it was radical to drop Mormonism and move to San Francisco and become an artist.

PETER DALE SCOTT

Peter Dale Scott believes in indeterminacy. He is a poet, former Canadian diplomat, and professor emeritus of English at the University of California, Berkeley, yet he will tell you that he did not—and still might not—entirely believe himself to be these things. It is fitting, then, that his poetry is political and his politics are somewhat poetic.

Scott's writings include a trilogy of book-length poems—*Coming to Jakarta, Listening to the Candle, Minding the Darkness*—and two-dozen nonfiction texts analyzing 9/11, the assassination of JFK, CIA corruption, and other points of contention in America's history involving what Scott has termed "deep politics."

What would you consider your first political experience?

Because my father was a politician, I was involved in party electoral politics from the age of twelve. But that wasn't me; that was just going with the flow. The first thing that was me, I think, was when I was a sophomore at McGill and The Red Dean of Canterbury—who was a dean of Canterbury and went to the Soviet Peace Congress and was passionately against nuclear weapons and in other words did everything that earned him the *soubriquet* "the Red Dean"—came. I had helped organize a club on campus for our social democratic party, the CCF, and we invited him to come and speak on campus. We were first told we could and then told we couldn't. So he spoke from a building off campus and we had loudspeakers outside, and then somebody came and cut the loudspeakers. So, you know, it was hardball. That got me riled up and, with four other people, we secretly met to organize a protest rally without a permit on the steps of the McGill Union just off campus.

Two of us were going to do the leafleting [but] the next morning at five o'clock it was pouring rain to the extent that you couldn't even pass out a leaflet. So I called my friend and I said, "It's off." Only, it wasn't off, because I went to the Union at noon, there was a row of police cars and a row of RCMP on horseback, enough to attract a crowd. Next thing you knew everyone was milling around saying, "What's happening," and the number of police cars doubled. For years I thought one of the five of us betrayed the meeting to the police, but now I think it's much more likely that we were wiretapped. Then in the end, there was a huge meeting of the Student Union, and I addressed that meeting and got a resolution of protest passed.

But I count another episode as more educational in terms of making me feel that you can make a difference. The minister of justice from the ruling Liberal Party spoke at McGill, and in the question period someone (maybe me, maybe not) asked why Japanese people in Canada had been interred during the war even though there was no evidence of treason among them. The minister replied vehemently to the effect that there was indeed evidence of such treason, concluding, "One of them was shot." So I wrote to one of the few CCF members of Parliament about this, and he asked about it in the Parliamentary Question Period, getting the answer that in fact there had never been any such shooting. I don't want to suggest that this made any significant difference, but at least I got the sense that government could be responsive to input from below.

What was activated in you?

I don't want to differentiate it in me too much but I certainly want to make a distinction between Canada and America. In Canada, national politics is something you feel responsible for, because it's on a much more human scale; whereas for most Americans politics is like the weather. It's something that goes on in the heavens and you're much less likely to imagine that you can do anything to affect it.

When was the first time you thought of yourself as a creative person?

I'm still not sure. I've written poetry since I was about ten. For the first half of my life, people would say, "Are you a poet?" and I'd say, "Well, I write poetry." Then just short of being fifty, which is a kind of crisis period in a person's development, I had hepatitis in England and was hospitalized and stared at a ceiling for two weeks. I couldn't eat, I couldn't move—it was that devastating. I lay there and decided that my life had to change, and from now on when people asked if I was a poet I was going to say yes. It's interesting that, having made that decision, no poems issued at first; but two years later, after another personal crisis, I started writing my poetic trilogy, *Seculum*.

I felt very undefined for the first half of my life. I played at being a diplomat, enjoyed it, but wasn't really a diplomat. And then, thank goodness, I got a job as a professor because of a PhD I hadn't really wanted to get. That was more than a joy, I loved it; but I didn't really feel like it was "me." I still feel undefined but now I'm living in the center of my un-definition and I feel that's where I belong. The best thing that ever happened to me was retiring, because I am now a full time writer for the first time in my life.

In terms of expressing political concerns through a creative medium, was that intuitive?

I don't decide on the poetry side, poems come. The part of you that writes poetry isn't the part of the brain that makes decisions. I think I write better politics because I write poetry, and more than one person has said to me that my method in political writing is more like an artist's method than a political scientist's method, which I take as a compliment. I think it's to do with intuition: If you have a crazy side thought, pursue it, don't stamp it out.

My style is quite digressive and that's why I have so many footnotes in my prose, because I go with those digressions, but I also feel that those digressions create a larger picture. What's bad about contemporary politics and poetry is too many linear narratives that aren't taking into account the counter-arguments that could conceivably reconcile them to the other person's position. As a former diplomat, I'm always aiming at that kind of reconciliation—quite explicitly. I think a dialogue that can reach the alienated on the right will be a stronger movement than one that, as at present, is mostly just reaching to the alienated on the left. I think Occupy themselves may think that, at least some of them.

How do you think imagination figures in American society at the moment?

I give good marks to America as a country as opposed to as a national government. As a country it is highly imaginative, highly creative, for good and for bad. We have all kinds of goofy religions, for example, and enormous creativity on an engineering level. You have asked a huge question and I think you've spotted me as someone who likes big questions and big answers. At present, in English-language poetry, I prefer American poetry to English, Canadian, or Australian. Not only that but Whitman—who is a poet I still have some problems with but obviously a great genius—I think his imagination sparked movements all over the world. And explicitly, in the case of Milosz, my model, who wrote in Polish but was very inspired by Whitman. Jazz is something else that took off and affected the whole world, so you don't have to be an upper middle class genius to do something really creative.

I think that we have to answer the question not in terms of averages or what the mass is like, but what is coming out of America as an entirety. I think there is a lot of creativity, a lot of imagination, and I think they overlap. A lot of imagination is passive, really, which is not to its discredit. People are contemplatives. You have a rediscovery of monasticism in America, which, to me, is very important. I've written about Thomas Merton, partly because both my first wife and second wife were Buddhists and I was dragged willy-nilly into Buddhism and am now quite committed to it. So I have a very large idea of creativity and imagination which includes just sitting in some little hut on the side of a hill. It's a comparative question, right? If we say, is America creative, do we mean more so than Nicaragua?

Perhaps I am asking whether imagination is present as an ideal in America?

For me imagination is not so much an ideal as it is a tool, a capacity. This gets into an issue I have with some modern poets. Dada was imaginative, but I don't think very great art. It had imagination at the cost of everything else. For me imagination by itself is not an ideal, but a world without imagination is certainly an anti-ideal, so imagination has to do with creating a better world. It will take imagination to have a better world, but my idea of a better world is not one where we're all just being imaginative.

What do you see when you look at contemporary American society?

It depends on the day of the week. There are many people I know and respect who are saying that America is finished as a country or that America is now an evil country and deserves anything that happens to it. There are still a few people who see America as the hope for the world. I think America at the time of the American Revolution *was* a new hope for the world. There's a word that's used a lot in this country to refer to this view of American history: exceptionalism. The idea that America is different and exceptional is very out of fashion now, but I do think that America *was* exceptional.

At this point, America is receding from its ambitious hopes for itself but it's not the first time that America has receded. I gave a talk recently saying America is experiencing a nightmare right now; but the first thing to add is that nightmares are something you wake up from, and the second thing to add is that I feel as though I've been through at least three nightmares since I first moved here in 1952. That was in the midst of McCarthyism, which was definitely a nightmare, and people thought 1984 had already arrived and that there would never be a free-thinking America again and that all turned out to be wrong. Then in Vietnam, things got very ugly. The war itself was ugly and the antiwar movement, as it became more and more combative and manipulative and violent, also became ugly. It was another nightmare but America got better.

I invented this little bit of rhetoric to cheer other people up. Does it cheer me up? I don't know. I cannot confidently predict that America will wake up. America rebounded from the Gilded Age of the nineteenth century and introduced reforms to reduce the gap between the rich and the poor, or as we now say, the 1 percent and the 99 percent. The question is, can that happen again now that the 1 percent are so much wealthier than they have ever been before? Because I believe in indeterminacy, I will never commit to either: "America will wake up and be better again" or, "America is finished." I'm not interested in that kind of judgment.

I think in China you would have more definite opinions about certain things. There's more polarization of power and powerlessness. But America is certainly in a period of crisis right now. It's economic, it's political, it's military, but I think above all it's moral and spiritual. I think there has been a corruption of spirituality in this country. I recently gave a talk on poetry and I quoted Milosz, when he talked about how "some basic confidence is needed, a sense of *open space ahead* of the individual and the human species." That's what Whitman gave America: [the idea] that America could and would and should be different.

When I refer to days of the week, I say I am a pessimist on Monday, an optimist on Tuesday, and a pessimist again on Wednesday. America attracts me because, unlike Canada, it's undetermined. It could go one way or another very easily, and frequently zigs and zags its way through its turbulent history.

You mustn't forget that America had a Civil War and before that it was thirteen very different states merging, and in the minds of some of those states they were each going to continue to be a state in a federation that was not a State. Lincoln changed that and now America is a State, and there's a lot of protest against that, which bubbles up in the Tea Party and left-wing anarchism. It's good, I think, that America is not totally committed to being a unitary State. I personally would like to see it be more of a federation of states.

Why is that?

Because so much of the anger and hatred in this country comes from people being forced to share the same laws to a greater extent than is necessary. I don't see why gun laws should be the same in Idaho and the District of Columbia. I would say: Let's have more tolerance of divergence of opinions. It is awkward if, in fact, you cross a state line and are suddenly under a different set of laws and penalties, so I'm not giving an ideal solution. But right now the left hate the Supreme Court, and the right hate the Supreme Court more than the left do. The Court is trying to get everyone to wear exactly the same kind of legal jacket and it's extremely painful. It causes a lot of hatred and a certain amount of rebellion. I'm not on the right but I am, to a certain extent, sympathetic to the Tea Party's desire of less central government direction.

Where does Occupy Wall Street sit amongst this?

The problem is that Occupy has defined itself as leaderless. The only way you can enforce anything is through General Assembly, which I think is not being realistic about the problems of organizing a mass movement that has very powerful forces aligned against it. By the way, I want to make it very clear that what I am saying now is not trying to give advice to Occupy because they are mostly young people and I am an old person; and when I was an organizer on the Berkeley campus, one of the things I really resented was older people coming to us and saying, "If you knew as much as I know . . ." so I'm just giving you my personal reaction.

I have to distinguish between Occupy East and Occupy West, and I am talking now about Occupy East. I think that everywhere Occupy wants to be nonviolent. The whole spirit of it, even the word, is: We just go and occupy. But you have to deal with the problem of provocateurs. I know, because I had to deal with them for twenty years. Sometimes when

I had a white armband and it was my special job I had people saying to me, "This isn't working, we have to get our guns." These people were obviously fake and had been sent to rile things up. Twenty years ago I underwent nonviolence training, to learn how to deal with these people, but you have to be trained and you have to have a strategy for it.

I suspect, in a very broad way, that Occupy will never seize the heart of America as a whole until it can deal with the question of nonviolence. It is going to produce sincere popular antagonism of the right if it becomes strong, just as the antiwar movement naively went out and said they were going to make people think, and they went out and made people think, and people—after thinking about it—elected Reagan.

This is something I haven't said about America yet but it needs to be said: Because America is not a nation in the traditional sense like Sweden or Norway or Switzerland, there is no real consensus as to what America should be. There is no real civil society on the national level. There are very strongly developed local senses of citizenship—very powerful; in Berkeley there is almost too much of it—and the point I am trying to get to is that in the absence of a consensus, there's a lot of striving; a lot of people who think, "We are the real America," and therefore that those people over there are not the real America, and so there's a lot of anger and hatred.

I think that America has not yet had the experience of arousing a major movement that didn't arouse a sense of resentment and hatred in the people who were not part of the movement, because there is no real touchstone to say what America is. What America is, will be decided 100 years from now. That is both the great opportunity of America, the open space ahead, and—I'll get a little prescriptive here—the need to be very cautious and charitable in any movement that you build.

I wrote a poem to the Tea Party. Ideas have consequences, and a Republican arranged for me to meet with the head of the local Tea Party. It was a very enjoyable lunch, but it was clear that there will be no reconciliation in that direction with this particular woman. Her role model is John Yoo, my colleague, a law professor at UC, who went to work in the Bush Administration and wrote what are called the Torture Memos. He's just written, in the *National Review*, an article saying that we need a much more forceful strategy to develop a case for invading Iran. So I say to this woman who says she wants less federal government, how on earth can you support John Yoo who tells the president in a memo that he can do anything he wants because he's commander in chief? And her response was, "I love John Yoo."

Frankly, I think America has gone insane at the center. They can't stop now. They have a strategy of dominating the world and this means they have to have bases everywhere. They used a base in Uzbekistan, then for a while they pulled out after [Islam] Karimov massacred a peaceful protest crowd of hundreds of people, and was reportedly boiling some of his enemies alive. That was too much even for the Bush Administration and they cancelled U.S. military aid. And now Obama is going to restore it! This is total insanity.

When you see these things so clearly, how do you maintain that sense of the open space ahead?

Well, you have to think big. You have to not be overwhelmed by what's happening here so that you forget what's happening over there. I've had times of crisis like the one in *Coming to Jakarta*, which I had right after the election of Reagan.

Seeing Reagan elected by a large majority and re-elected by an even larger majority made me think that maybe I am totally out of touch with this country and what I see in its future is not what's there. But of course in the case of Bush, George W., it's doubtful he was elected by the American people. But they allegedly re-elected him and that was hard. So I have times when I wonder, and then there are times when I am absolutely sure, that my real hope is more for a better Canada than a better America. But Canada for me is not the place to do it. Canada has wonderful movements and I could be very happy there, but right now we have a Tory P.M., Stephen Harper, whose main ideal is to do what America wants.

I lose hope from time to time. I have lost it in the past, and working all that out took a whole long poem to get it back. But I think a realistic sense of hope is probably one which from time to time faces the risk of extinction. People who are just naively hopeful are probably not much use.

MARINA SITRIN

Marina Sitrin is a postdoctoral fellow at the CUNY Graduate Center's Committee on Globalization and Social Change and holds a PhD in global sociology from Stony Brook University. She has edited *Horizontalism: Voices of Popular Power in Argentina*, containing interviews about the non-hierarchical methods of organizing she witnessed during the popular uprisings, which began in 2001 and have continued in various forms.

Sitrin describes herself as "a writer, lawyer, teacher, organizer and dreamer," but I would suggest that in her capacity as "dreamer," she is working to shift society's perception of the term "realist."

❦

Tell me about your activism.

I have always been a political activist, since I was in middle school. I come from an interracial family, so some of my siblings are half-black and my family is Jewish but secular. Thinking about society and racism, I grew up with a sense of seeking justice, but what that justice looks like has always been a question.

In 1994 I learnt about the Zappatistas and while that did a little bit and I was inspired by them, it wasn't until my last year in law school: I was in the International Womens' Human Rights clinic at CUNY which is a year-long clinic, with some amazing thinkers using human rights law to really push the boundaries of what's possible. I went to the Seattle protest as part of MADRE, the women's human rights organization. When I got to Seattle, even the human rights organizations were saying, "No new round, turnaround," which meant to not engage and that people needed to stop the meetings. I had been an activist and I knew there was activism going on in the street so I made a decision not to go to the meetings as part of MADRE and to turn in my NGO card and join the blockades.

While Seattle was still national, it was a moment of thinking about the world as one world. The forms of organization in Seattle for me were transformative. I'd been, at different times, in different socialist groups and always had a critique: I was kicked out of one, was told I had anarchist tendencies in another, then I was told I was a "movementist"—I don't know what that means except that I like movements, but I felt like I wanted to be organized. So what do you do if you have a critique of capitalism and you want to be organized? Who else is organizing? What does that look like?

I'd read about the Paris Commune and all of these worker soviets, then I went to my first spokescouncil in Seattle and it was an "Aha!" moment: what I've been reading about really can happen and that gut feeling I had about political parties, that that is not the way we should be organizing . . . my world kind of broke open. Fortunately I was going into my last semester of law school because I came back from Seattle and helped to organize the Direct Action Network in New York and at the same time began to organize activist legal collectives. Everything changed for me.

You have a PhD in sociology and have participated actively in movements both here and internationally. How did your study of sociology and your experience in actual situations intersect?

Latin American and European sociologists lend themselves to what's happening in the world with social movements. I met some amazing people at Stony Brook and am privileged to have worked with them, but U.S. social movement framework is still fairly rigid. They all use this contentious politics framework, which is that you have to meet certain guidelines to be a social movement, but, also, it says that you have to be in a contentious relationship with some sort of institutional power. The problem is that the more autonomous movements in Argentina, or, say, the Zappatistas in Chiapas and so many of the Occupy movements, don't fall into that framework because they're not positioning themselves in relation to the State or institutional power. It's not that they don't take the State seriously, but they're positioning themselves in relationship to one another.

What [sociology] made me much more conscious of was the power of the academy in relationship to social movements. It's actually more powerful—more dangerous *or* more useful—than I realized. I used to call intellectuals who wrote about social movements *socialista de café*, you know, armchair socialists who would write about movements. In my experience in Argentina, there are some social movement thinkers who are very well respected in the United States who after maybe two years of looking at the movements in Argentina, because [the movements] didn't take power, dismissed them and did a great disservice to them by only looking at it through their particular lens. People say to me all the time, "Oh, people are still doing things in Argentina?" and it's remarkable because there are hundreds of assemblies right now up and down the Andes and they're all using direct democracy and *horizontalidad*. It's not what people had hoped it would be in 2001, but it's hardly dead.

I think I learned more that the academy can play a bad role, so I am now trying to figure out what my role is as a movement person and an intellectual, balancing movement writing with sometimes trying to intervene in the world of scholarly publications to make sure that the historical record is correct. Even though things are changing a lot, history is still often written by a small group of people who dominate the narrative and they're not usually the people making history.

I know that you were involved with Occupy essentially from its inception.

If I were going to do markers, it was a moment like Seattle and Argentina. Those first assemblies in Tompkins Square Park, I could tell something was different. I had no idea what it would look like nationally or even that we'd occupy in New York. There were fifty, sixty, seventy people sitting in a circle struggling really hard with a form of consensus that was new to most people, but really dedicated to trying to create direct democracy and really trying to listen to each other and create an open space. Starting in mid-August it was amazing to see how people were beginning to organize in working groups. Some young people were going out to sleep overnight on Wall Street to see what would happen.

What happened?

They got arrested. They were doing speeches in front of the George Washington monument, and were trying to test the Bloombergville law by sleeping on the sidewalk and blocking traffic. They were released fairly quickly and I think the charges didn't ultimately stick. It's quite funny to watch them talking to the police, because they filmed themselves, explaining how they have a right to do it. These are people who are really young and post-inequality and post- so many things in the system, but who at the same time believed, I think, in a lot of what the system tells us. By that I mean laws and the Constitution. On the one hand they are protesting because society is not just, and then when they're arrested they're shocked and outraged that their First Amendment right to speech and protest is being violated. This is correct, but their frustration does not extend to the law and the police. I think that's part of the radicalization that happened with people during Occupy: feeling as though they, or we, don't have the future we were promised but still expecting that our rights would be respected. So when they were brutalized and arrested unlawfully, people were shocked that the police were enforcing laws that didn't apply or didn't exist. It was an interesting contradiction.

What is your understanding of how people came to the point of occupying?

On the one hand, I don't know. On the other, because I have spent time in Chiapas and Greece and Argentina, people say such similar things around the world, where you kind of reach this level of frustration that is actually not anger. There's this idea that they're *indignados* in Spain and they say, "No we're not! That's just what the media calls us, we're determined." The Zappatistas say, "Yabasta!" and in Argentina they say, "Que Se Vayan Todos! (They all must go!)" It's just like, enough! There's an exclamation point because it's an exclamation of just, "Ahhh! I've had it! What do I do?"

So people go out in the street and find each other. That's not a scientific answer and it wouldn't fit in a social science box, but it's just a point that people reach. I don't just think, I *know*, that in times of crisis—Rebecca Solnit talks about this in *A Paradise Built in Hell*—earthquakes, natural disaster, people come out and try to find each other. We're not at that level yet and they're not there yet in Greece, but the level of frustration gets so high when people feel as though they're not represented and don't have a voice that they come out of their homes and stay out and take this direct action that is huge.

I can't totally explain it; it's an emotion, it's an exclamation, and people find support in that shared exhale. I think we learn from each other globally, I don't know how exactly. It's not like in the 1960s with spreading "the revolution." In Latin America they use the language of contagion, like a virus. It's not an intentionally spread something but there's an idea: You know somewhere back in history workers occupied somewhere and it was democratic, so somehow that gets into our beings. Some people probably had a very good idea and studied what happened before September 17, but some people who were there only had a very vague idea. It's somewhere in our imagination and I think that played a role. We know that people have done this before.

The key is that it presents people with another possibility. It allows people to believe in an alternative.

And also to see the positive. I think people are inspired by seeing the positive. The idea that things have to be so horrible before action can be taken, I don't think is true. In Athens, it's bad like young people can't afford to move out from their parents' homes. It's not like they're starving. It's a different level. It's the possibility that mobilizes people but the potential for negative possibility mobilizes them too, which I think is interesting. It's not a coincidence that people believe—probably rightly so—that they're going to benefit from things continuing the way that they are, so things changing for them would be less concrete. They're not the same as so many people who have been organizing who have college degrees and now can't get a job, or the future they thought they had they don't actually have.

To participate in a movement like Occupy also presents people with the opportunity for participation, which I don't think is part of most people's everyday experience.

Not at all, and I think that's the hierarchy, when the rules of behavior are rigidly determined by someone else. The nature of being horizontal and creating these open, directly democratic spaces means everyone participates. Doing that means creating together because there's not a "party line" or a direction led by one person. Everyone *needs* to participate. And that's what people love about these movements: It's regular people coming together and figuring out everything from how they're going to run an assembly to how they're going to pick up trash.

In other places around the world it's become more sophisticated so it becomes about schools and health care. In Argentina, they're running hundreds of workplaces together so it has to be creative but they also have structures that allow it to be creative and for everyone to be heard. That's what people crave and why they keep coming back.

At the core, this experience of direct democracy is going to stay with people. And what that looks like, if we become millions of people in assembly creating a parallel system instead of the system we live under, would be fantastic and I think it will happen over a long history. I think these seeds of participation, our creativity, doesn't just go away. They use the saying, "You can't evict an idea," and it's also that you can't evict this experience. People in Argentina said this as well: "I am now a historical subject. I am now an actor in my life." You feel like your voice matters, and it does, so why would you go home again and have someone tell you what to do?

MICHAEL PARENTI

There is a wall in author Michael Parenti's study covered with photographs, posters, newspaper clippings, and memorabilia from the innumerable protests and demonstrations he has participated in. At one point in our interview, he illustrated an anecdote with a picture of himself, head split open, during the Kent State rally in 1970.

Parenti is a virulent critic of American social, economic, and political institutions. He insists not only on the recognition of a dire set of circumstances, but a radical reconsideration of the way we think about the idea of circumstances in the first place. His published works include *Democracy for the Few* (now in its ninth edition) and *Contrary Notions: The Michael Parenti Reader*.

At what point did you become intensely involved in politics?

I got intensely involved in political life after I got my PhD [in political science from Yale University]. I was a political scientist and teaching, and I suddenly got very troubled about the Vietnam War. I raised questions about that war and the answers I got—in correspondence with Vice President Hubert Humphrey—made me realize that U.S. leaders were pursuing that war with serious and knowing intent. The war wasn't a mistake; it was what they wanted to be doing. So then I started raising questions about the people who got us into that war, and then I started raising questions about the leadership and perspective and ideology—and the system that produced such decision-makers.

I repeatedly discovered that I was not so radical; it was that other people were so conservative. I was constantly considered to be way far-out and extremist. I thought, what's extremist about not wanting to have our rulers napalming villages in which other people live happily and quietly halfway around the world? The extremists are the individuals in the planes and the people ordering the planes out on their deadly missions, and the people who want to kill me as a traitor because I'm questioning such things. And of course I wasn't a lone, courageous dissident. We had hundreds of thousands of people marching. Some of my leftist consciousness that emerged during the Vietnam era was a product of what you'd call a reverse socialization. As a professor I was learning from some of the student organizations. They were writing about things that I had never heard about and questioning things that my colleagues had never bothered to question. As I say, I got more and more involved. I got involved physically, got beaten up.

What happened there?

I'll show you a picture. [The black and white photograph shows Parenti in a chaotic crowd, the back of his head clearly bloodied]. That's me, with my head all busted open. The state troopers were up on a wall and we were down in the driveway, and one state trooper was coming down with his club to hit me directly on top of my head, a blow that can kill you. I heard him say later in the jail, "If I'd got a good clean lick on that guy he'd be a dead man." This was at the University of Illinois during the Kent State uprisings. They threw me in jail for two days and the whole campus—10,000 people—went out on a strike.

What was it in people, or in you, that was activated to the extent that you were willing to . . .

Put your body on the line? I think it was really the feeling that every day people were getting killed in large numbers in Vietnam and Cambodia and Laos.

Although we're still aware of versions of that reality, that period has never been replicated.

Well, we have something like it with the Occupy movement, and authorities are being as repressive as ever. At some point when everyone has been feeling alone and powerless, suddenly there is this remarkable resurgence. To have this resurgence of visible demonstrations, likeminded collectivities, really has an impact. It fortifies, it energizes. People coalesce together out in the street. They bring democracy into the streets and give it visibility. These demonstrations are replicated in communities around the world, which has an interesting impact.

And then there's this wonderful ideological device of "1 percent versus 99 percent." I mean, for those of us who have spent forty years talking about the great class divide, only to be ignored and dismissed as "extremist," this was a remarkable ideological advance for the activist left. There's no country in the world like the United States when it comes to having class analysis denied and muffled and muted. Americans don't even know what class is. You can show a bunch of Americans a movie about class division and they'll say, "Well, gee, there was racism in there." They're taught not to see class so they don't see class. They only think of class as a demographic trait, which is not the way race and gender should be treated either. They are dynamics of oppression and division and they often serve the overall class power system. You can get writings relating class to divorce patterns or class to education, income, and lifestyle, but what you don't get is class as a social relation; class as a small group of people controlling the resources of society at the expense of others, class as a dynamic of wealth and power. And here, this is what you were getting with the Occupy movement. It was adversarial: 1 percent versus 99 percent. I thought that was a great ideological victory. You even heard commentators picking it up: "How does the 99 percent . . ."

What exactly is the ideological victory? What does it do for people when they're able to see class?

They're able to see it not as difference in income but as a social relationship whereby the land, labor, resources, control of media, control of the corporations that are privatizing our universities. They see it in operation and they see its oppressive nature. They see how people are suffering terribly in a broken, exploitative health system where the function is to produce immense profits. In the old days, you would just be dismissed as a Marxist if you talked about the "great class divide" that exists in the world and in our country. To finally understand that there is a small yet enormously powerful coterie presiding over corporate America, determining how we live, the images in our head, the quality of the air we breathe, the food we eat, and the water we drink so that they can get away with as much as they can, to understand how really at war those people are with us, and how we have to wake up and do something about it, that's a terrific breakthrough.

This is one of the most successfully repressed countries in the world. I was in London and I heard the leader of this big Trotskyite convention say, "I don't think all Americans are stupid but most of them certainly are." But it's not stupidity. It's a far superior and more intelligent ruling class. This empire is winning success after success. At the same time the idiot liberals and the idiot Democrats get up and say, "This empire is ruining us, it's terrible, we shouldn't get involved here. It's outrageous." It's not outrageous! It's perfectly rational. They say, "Our leaders are so stupid, so inept, so driven by messianic foolishness." No. You're stupid when you think the people who own the world are stupid. That's the extent of the liberal critique? For those of us who have a radical analysis instead of just a liberal complaint, it's a very hard ideological struggle. To suddenly see tens of thousands of people in different communities talking about the 1 percent, to be saying the things we've been struggling with for years, that was a very nice breakthrough.

There's one thing that ruling interests do throughout history: They don't leave to chance the control of discourse and ideology. Just a few years ago, we had the bicentennial of the French Revolution. You would have thought we had the guillotines right outside. This was a great democratic revolution during which Europe witnessed the end of 2,000 years of autocracy and absolutism and inquisitions and feudal lordships. People rose up and overthrew the decadent, exploitative aristocracy. And all we get are these stories about the supposedly bloodthirsty Robespierre who led the Terror, and who, by the way, was a great popular leader.

There's a most telling quote from Mark Twain, from his novel *A Connecticut Yankee in King Arthur's Court*. He said that there are two terrors: the first is the terror that we hear about, of the angry populace delivering retribution upon those who made them suffer. The victims of that terror are counted carefully and they number in the hundreds, maybe sometimes several thousands, and their perpetrators are endlessly denounced while they are reverently remembered. Then there's the terror of the *Ancien Régime*, the terror endured by the millions who live and die in starvation, stupefied by cold and lack of adequate education. They die so that these few at the top can live with every conceivable luxury. The victims of the *Ancien Régime*'s terror, they number in the millions, but their numbers are never counted.

How would you describe American society at present?

I see a society that is suffering horrible distorting effects in its food supplies, in its transportation, in its health system, in its housing markets.

You have people buying up these mortgaged-out houses and you have other people living in vans who used to live in these houses. I see a society that is terribly disordered—not because people are confused or stupid. In fact, they may be catching wise. But our society is terribly distorted because the 1 percent is able to control the resources of power.

Which is more effective in mobilizing people: desire for something better or discontent with the present?

It's a combination of anger and hope. Anger, when you awaken, you see how bad it is, but there's some feeling that others also see it, and a momentum begins to develop. The ruling interests have to work pretty hard, you know. One of their goals is to deflect your justifiable grievances toward irrelevant enemies. They will teach you to blame your grievances on the illegal immigrants, on the "cultural elites." So the reactionaries create a false conservative populism, just as Hitler did with the Germans. The Germans had very real grievances, but to move against the unfair tax burden and the cartels controlling them would have been to move in a genuinely revolutionary direction. Instead, they got deflected toward irrelevant enemies: the trade unionists, the Jewish bankers, the communists. That was a great way of deflecting their otherwise legitimate grievances. That's what the Tea Party idiots are doing. A lot of them have been screwed over and they know something's wrong, but they have had their grievances successfully deflected toward irrelevant enemies.

Let's talk about hope. What is the difference between hope and idealism?

The problem is that it's often hard to keep your hope up. I can't reveal how despairing I sometimes feel about the way things go, that you've got ruling-class leaders who are taking all of us on a bus ride off a cliff and their profit-driven interest is to run up and down the aisle trying to sell seatbelts to us. They do suffer from a profit pathology, it's just crazy. So it's hard to maintain hope. But idealism is that state of mind that impels you to act regardless of whether there are grounds for optimism or pessimism. You act because it's the right thing to do. And, being the right thing to do, the question of whether acting is effective or ineffective is secondary because it's the only thing you can do. You see whole bunches of people acting out against all sorts of odds, and doing it because they're outraged. You can see that hope stirs up your ideals and your ideals incite your hope. And sometimes your idealism actually carries you to victory.

Do you believe that hope is something that can mobilize people?

Yes. Certainly when people feel that something is important and it's urgent and it's needed and it can be done, that mobilizes them.

This is a quote from John Berger: "a protest is not a sacrifice made for some alternative, more just future, but an inconsequential redemption of the present." What do you think of that idea?

If your protest is only motivated by a sense that it will be immediately consequential then there isn't much protesting for you to do. During the Vietnam era and later on, with the Iraq war, there was no shortage of people who said, "What makes you think you're going to stop this war by marching in the street with a sign?" Writing a letter to your congressman, getting arrested, getting yourself all beat up, what makes you think you're going to stop the war? And the truth is, they're absolutely right. None of those things is going to stop the war. But all of them taken together did have an impact. It reached the point in the mid '70s where the U.S. Army wasn't fighting anymore. And it was because those guys were picking up on the strong antiwar sentiments coming from the home front. They would not make contact with the enemy. They'd sit by the roadside. There were a number of mutinies too, but they weren't called mutinies. The military brass was very smart: They quieted the resistors in their ranks instead of putting them on trial, because of the publicity such rebellion would get. All this resistance was arising in the military ranks because the public had changed. Nobody was supporting that war anymore except a few nuts in the White House. Nixon's B-52 bombers were getting shot down because his coders weren't coding new paths for them, so they'd continue on the same path and get shot down by the Vietnamese. Protest was immensely consequential. Soon after that they decided they could not have a conscripted army and would have to have a professional volunteer army, who would be less susceptible to refusing to perform.

Is it reasonable to expect change? To expect an alternative from what we have now?

I would say that it's not likely we can expect change, but we have to fight for it. In fact, that's the only thing we are to do. The problem is that those who want change don't have the power, and those who have the power don't want change. I've said before that these guys wouldn't believe climate change is happening until the North Pole melts. Well, the North Pole is melting. The Arctic is absolutely crashing down. It's even destroying the Gulf Stream that keeps Europe a temperate zone. What is corporate America doing? They're thinking about new opportunities for profiting from the meltdown. New oil reserves are becoming accessible for drilling. The Northwest Passage is a dream that goes back to Lewis and Clark, or back to Columbus and Henry Hudson. With the ice caps melting there is now a Northwest Passage opening up. There are companies forming to show others how they can make money from global warming. So they're not thinking of change, they're thinking only of operational opportunity for profit maximization.

Are these parameters that we're always going to have to work within, that those who want change don't have power?

Well, sometimes somebody wants power and he really believes in fundamental change, like Chavez in Venezuela. He has a piece of State power; he's no dictator. He won five out of six national democratic elections or referenda. He's actually bringing in changes. I was down there, reporting on it. There are people seeing dentists who have never been able to see a dentist in their lives. Every so often, somebody breaks through in some way. But whether he survives or not is still open to question. So, it doesn't always happen, but there are examples now and then.

DANA DART-McLEAN

Dana Dart-McLean is an artist and writer. Her work has been exhibited at Small A Projects in Portland, Nicolai Wallner in Copenhagen, and Western Exhibitions in Chicago, among others.

Dart-McLean is also the co-founder, with Brian Mumford, of Occupation/Preoccupation, a project in which American musicians record covers of songs from regions where America maintains military bases. There are over 700 of these bases. One recently covered song was a recommendation from Zainab Alkhawaja, an activist in Bahrain and the daughter of human rights activist Abdulhadi Alkhawaja.

Do you identify as being political?

I do, but I definitely come at it through the feminist maxim, "the personal is political," and think of it as one of the framing dynamics that shape experience and interpersonal connection. So I think about it as being really integrated into life and something that is always happening.

What do you think it means to be politically active?

I would think it means having a moral framework that you have deeply considered and that you believe to be true, and engaging with other people and power dynamics through that framework. My grandmother is a peace activist—or she was. She had been arrested for protesting every conflict the U.S. has been involved with. Her activism began in Australia when she was living there; they went back because my grandfather owed the government for putting him through school in Chicago and had to go back to teach in Perth. My grandmother got really interested in native Australian aboriginal struggles and through that became a member of Women's International League for Peace and Freedom, an organization that Jane Addams started. Through that involvement she became a really committed antiwar activist, protesting the Vietnam War. She had all these experiences that have always been part of our family legacy, so that as a way of understanding political engagement has always been part of my experience. She had a little note on her computer, which was the Jewish saying, *tikkun olam*: "You do not have to complete the task, neither can you put it down."

I feel as though, in this time, we are presented with many opportunities to avoid even a general sense of social responsibility.

I think that right now in this country and in my generation, because of how consumer-oriented many public spaces have become, the space that's open for people conceptually and psychologically is to be more responsible to your friend group and your scene and your tastes. I see a lot of the same characteristics and behaviors [as social responsibility] but just directed toward the music that someone's into, for example. That can still be a very devotional way to live, it's just not social in a humanist tradition way where you think of the collective and what would be good for future generations.

There is potential also in the merging of both kinds of behaviors; of, as you said, the political returning to the personal. Where does awareness fit into this?

I think the last 150 years have been kind of a series of emerging global planetary consciousness crises. If I can use ultra–West Coast ways of talking, I believe there are these successive levels of awareness, through war and nuclear development and exploitative mass relationships, of finite resources. The scenario is, I think, being expressed in people's consciousness and the social consciousness in a lot of different ways. I think people are being encouraged to study their personal devotion to taste and style, and that [politics] is still really a part of consciousness, it's just that a lot of people express it through despair or assuming a victim role.

In the Portland Occupy there would be long sessions in the General Assembly where people would get up and tell their story of how they'd been victimized by the economic system and how it felt really good to finally have a forum where they could express this, that it was cathartic. I think it will develop into a more nuanced critique that begins with these expressions and moves to a much larger perspective. But there's an urgency to it that is really felt in the way people approach it, because people see that the current situation is totally unsustainable.

What do you see when you look at American society?

I am really privileged to exist in this tiny part of American culture that is a music, art, food, politics subculture, and which is really very positive and self-aware. Whenever I experience more mass-cultural things like corporate jobs or institutionalized health care, I find that there's a lot of averaging of individuals. You get this median-based option that really fits no one.

I feel as though there's passive resistance going on all the time where people are essentially committing suicide by making themselves morbidly obese and making themselves catatonic through watching hours and hours of television and surfing the Internet. I think of those behaviors as forms of resistance to a system that facilitates a totally unequal power dynamic. And I really appreciated that about the Occupy movement, that it was making economic disparity visible by showing the numbers. It recontextualizes a lot of these behaviors that are easy to see as negative personal values: laziness, greediness, all these things. This may be an out-there way of looking at it, but I think that those behaviors are forms of assuming personal power that, to me, is about a desire for change. Teenage cutters are a good example. They're turning the negation on to themselves, and taking control of those systems of pain.

For a long time I felt depressed and angry, and that interfered with my appreciation and celebration of the communities that are available if you're willing to set aside time to get your culture through showing up to where these small groups of people are. I've been a part of that way of getting culture pretty much my whole life, because my parents have always been interested in that stuff too. For a while I was down on it and I didn't like myself and other people who were part of it because it seemed indulgent, so I turned away.

What does the absence of culture do to people?

It's an interesting time for that because there's so much more possibility to be atomized or separate, and people are very much in this moment of worshipping the autonomous individual who doesn't have any need for other people. A computer is a good symbol for that. It's an autonomous thinking device that doesn't require interaction; it is complete and has everything inside of it.

What hope do you have for change?

On the one hand, I was teaching an art class and my co-teacher wanted to get frames from Ikea and, walking through the Ikea warehouse with 700 pine frames stacked to the ceiling, and then that multiplied by the amount of stores they have, and it's all going to be garbage in thirty years . . . I thought, "We are so fucked."

But at the same time, I feel trusting of people to experience greater awareness through things that happen around them, to be dynamic and to change. I think there is a lot of potential that we don't have any control over. So that remains open, and I also feel that my sense of hope and my sense of optimism doesn't negate my responsibility to behave morally. There's still a requirement. This is something that everyone has to come to, that there's still a responsibility to try to stop power dynamics that are oppressive. But it's complicated in this country because it's so hard to get accurate information.

There's a way that the power systems in this country are invested in people being ignorant, because otherwise Americans, or anyone . . . nobody wants children to be murdered and that is the daily reality of the places where we're engaging in explicit and covert operations. That's not a story that's widely available. There's a connection between this and the consumer identity, where people are not told the story of how the stuff they're buying gets to them.

Ikea just seemed like an example of how that structure of creating things on a mass scale is inherently violent. Communities are social structures that are small, so in order to make these massive uniform facilities where you can get identical products here as you can in Germany, communities have to be destroyed. There's a level of violence that goes into it which is not sustainable.

How do you situate yourself amongst this?

I have to recognize, like everyone, my limited and tiny existence and try to find ways to participate and things to do that I feel good about. For me, that has involved art and activism and community engagement.

CRAIG CALHOUN

Craig Calhoun is a professor of the social sciences at New York University and is the founding director of NYU's Institute for Public Knowledge. He has been president of the Social Science Research Council for over a decade. He has also been appointed the next director of the London School of Economics and Political Science. His published works include *Neither Gods Nor Emperors: Students and the Struggle for Democracy in China* and, most recently, *The Roots of Radicalism: Tradition, the Public Sphere, and Early 19th Century Social Movements*.

Calhoun told me, "You can keep distinct your analyses of empirical facts and your evaluations of them, but being a citizen shapes what you care about. The fact that I study social movements and protests and social change is shaped by the fact that I am also a citizen. They are interrelated."

<hr/>

How would you describe an American person's present experience of society?

I think it is of confusion. I think the average American is patriotic and attached to the idea of America, "the Nation," the society as a whole, and is resentful of the central government's interference in their life and of the large-scale institutions. They feel disempowered and controlled by those things. Some people put a left-wing spin on it, some a right-wing spin on it, but the widespread sentiment is that too much is happening with national government and corporations that is removed from us ordinary people. But, at the same time, [there is] an identification with the whole, either: we all have responsibilities to try to make the society better so we should all do something about racism and militarism, or: we should all embrace America—love it or leave it—we should be loyal to the society as a whole. It depends on the mood people are in, what they hold as their example, and to some extent people sort themselves out into left and right over these things, but with complicated relations. To the extent that the average American isn't just a statistical artifact and that there are commonalities, the commonalities are to do with both caring a lot about community and being likely to insist on a very individualistic view of themselves.

You have said that turbulent change can affect how people perceive themselves in society and how society perceives itself. Is it possible to see how that perception has changed?

At one level it's always dangerous to generalize about that; to say, "This is what happened," as if it's one change. Sometimes it's not a commonality but the issues that divide us that come to the fore. The '60s didn't just issue in people saying, "Peace and freedom," it also shaped some of the revitalization of the religion and politics that came after it, which wasn't what people were doing in the '60s exactly. [Something new emerged] partly out of spiritual seekings in the '60s, partly out of those getting "saved" from the '60s, [among] the number of people who turned to religion for an alternative framework in the wake of drug experiences or chaotic family experiences and the like. So it's not necessarily that there's just one direction or change that comes out of these things.

In the current context, something like inequality coming into focus in terms of how we see ourselves is interesting. America has long been a relatively unequal society compared to other nation-states, yet only in recent years has it become a theme of continuous conversation. The conversations don't all take the form of disagreement that it's either good or bad, but the issue is there. Partly due to Hurricane Katrina, partly due to the financial crisis and the crystallization of the 99 percent, it seems a widespread concern whatever you think about it. You can say that issue has come into focus in terms of how Americans understand themselves without saying all Americans have become equalitarian or anti-equalitarian.

How much of knowledge is experiential?

All, at some level, but the kinds of experiences are very different. Even the most immediately experiential—emotional dramas, very intense experience—is mediated by language and by what you've read or seen in the movies. We are deeply shaped by our personal experiences. Whole generations are shaped by common experiences; they change how we filter and use knowledge, but at the same time, it's sort of a chicken and egg question. The way we have those experiences, which we think of as personal experience, is shaped by experiences of how we saw our parents behave or what happened to us previously and then shaped by scripts or ideals, what we think ought to happen, what we think ought not to happen.

It's the same thing for political protests. One of the points I make in analyzing the Tiananmen Square protest is that people have ideas of something like how to organize a protest march, which are shaped by previous protest marches they've been in, ones that they've seen in the movies or read about in books, and they draw on the repertoire of those ideas in order to do something. It's not just that people happen to find themselves in the streets because they feel angry, there's a certain call for other people who feel angry to join them at a certain place, at a certain time, so the role of social media and personal conversation comes in. Then, having an image of what it would mean, having had the image of people gathered in Tiananmen Square, people in other countries gather.

Tell me about where education sits with what we're talking about.

There's the ability to be articulate, which depends on things like how many words you know, but then there's politics as, in itself, an educational process, and this idea is most associated with John Dewey, whom I very much agree with. If you think politics is just expressing the opinions you already have, either verbally or by voting, you have an impoverished conception of politics compared to entering into a process in which you can be educated, participate in your self-education, and participate in the education of others by debate, by gathering and discussing ideas, by trying to affect change, by seeing how things turn out well or turn out poorly. Sometimes failure is educational, [so are] successes that turn out to be too small.

The act of getting involved, the experience but also the reflection on that experience, is educational. The communication with other people is educational, [as is] the capacity to connect that to what you already know. The education is partly through connecting the particular immediate experience, the movement you're participating in and the issue you're confronting, to a bigger picture. And I do think it's a collective self-education that democracy, in particular, depends on.

You've spoken about the need for people to evaluate in terms of ideals and in terms of ultimate values and ultimate aims. That, to me, seems like part of a steep, uphill process.

Trying to live according to your highest ideals is hard and trying to live according to the highest possible ideals is even harder, because it involves learning more about everything until eventually you've set an unreachable goal. So I think that idealism can be understood as perfection and then a really steep path to how much of that perfection you can get, but I would emphasize something else: Each of us has aspirations beyond where we are right now and what we are like right now. I think that we can be engaged in fairly small ways that reach beyond where we are now. We have that capacity to reach beyond ourselves and we can harness that and recognize that in varying degrees.

That seems to require the reconciliation of parts of ourselves that are less than ideal, in a way.

It enables reconciliation to the less than ideal if we believe we have some hope of improving on it. It would be terribly depressing—it's bad enough to know that we have all these bad qualities as well as good qualities—if we thought we couldn't change any of them, if we thought we couldn't do anything about it.

Although I feel as though the two, at times, have to be held in balance. In the context of a movement, commitment has to be made despite the parts of it that you don't necessarily like.

I think that's true beyond movements, at the level of whole countries. We often have a challenge reconciling ourselves to the complexity, diversity, and sometimes disagreeableness of society in its larger sense: figuring out how to love it and what to change in it, how to be invested in it, to care enough about the other people, so that society is not just an abstraction to you, but then how to deal with the fact that those other people say things you don't like. This is a tension we all confront. What is really important is to accept and attach ourselves to the existing society, to life as it is around us, and at the same time not have a view that that's all there can be. I don't just mean [the belief] that there could be transcendence in a religious sense, but that [society] could be changed and we could make some things better. The balance is important. If you have a purified, idealized view of yourself or a movement it can be disempowering. It's the acceptance of your faults coupled with the recognition that you can try to improve on them, that makes for being relatively healthy as a person but also able to engage in collective action.

At any scale of collective action, there will be people who have slightly different priorities or want to try different tactics and you may try to organize and get an agreement but at some level, working with other people means accepting difference. However, if you start saying, "Let's just all get together and have a hug," that is disempowering. You have to take it seriously at some level.

I love the word "reconciliation"; it's one of the many that has been drawn from a religious vocabulary into a movement vocabulary. Most people will use that word without remembering the religion, although some of them will. It reflects the extent to which a religious message, like a movement message, is in part about what there is beyond the most immediate conditions we find ourselves in. The idea of reconciliation is at its best, is most helpful to us, when we think of a process and not just a fact.

You have said that one of the problems with the word "crisis" is that it suggests that a resolution, or reconciliation, will become clear at some point shortly after a "crisis" is declared. How do we continue to feel motivated in the presence of ambiguity?

In one way, ambiguity reflects openness and the potential for different things to happen. If everything were clearly determined you would have no choice and no capacity for action. So the very idea of action suggests that the world is ambiguous enough that things could turn out differently depending on what you do, yet people want assurances that when they do things the right thing will happen. You know, if you have the revolution there will be peace and truth and justice. Well, damn, we had the revolution and a bunch of bureaucratic apparatchik came to power. So it's the nature of action in general, especially dramatic social change and large-scale collective action, that you don't control everything that can happen. If you create so much assurance, you won't be able to act.

There are theories that deal with this in ways that are almost contradictory. Marxism, for example, says, "Workers, don't worry. History is on your side. There is going to be a collapse of capitalism; there's going to be a revolution and good things will come of this . . . but, you actually have to get out on the barricades! And you have to act! You have to do something!" There's a determined, reassuring knowledge that you will succeed but you have to do something. And those are in tension.

This is similar to the religious idea that God knows everything, God has *decreed*, but you actually have to do something. You have to affect some sort of change by praying. I think what this reveals to us is that we desire, on the one hand, the reassurance of an orderly, predictable world in which you can know what's going on and, on the other hand, freedom. Those things are really in some tension with each other. You wouldn't want a world in which there was such chaotic, complete randomness to what was going on, where everybody was free all the time and couldn't even control their freedom by saying, "I'm going to discipline myself now in order to have something else later." That extreme of freedom would not be self-empowerment. It would be, you know, being at the mercy of your whims and your environment. Conversely, a completely orderly, predictable, determined world would have no freedom.

So, the human predicament is precisely ambiguity: outcomes you can't control, unintended consequences of the actions you choose, and having to coordinate with other people you can only partially coordinate with. It ought to be the case that we embrace ambiguity, but we feel frustrated by it and we sort of resent it even though it's the reality of the milieu in which we live.

One of the biggest obstacles to movements is the sense that you can't do anything to change things. It's very disempowering to have a deterministic theory yet it's very frustrating to imagine a completely voluntaristic theory. People try it; it doesn't happen. They get disappointed but they also turn out to have ten different things they want. The challenge of getting a movement organized is of confronting the ambiguity and prioritizing. You can come to some agreement with other people about the priorities and this makes it look possible; if you can't, then it's not possible. Then you may have lots of people who are unhappy or anxious, occasionally protesting, but you won't get a movement.

Why is it powerful to recognize, to use your word, the "interconnectedness" of history?

I think we are all interconnected, all the time, and there's something powerful in recognizing that. The question is not, "To connect or not to connect?" The question is, "How are we connected?" So, that's powerful. Once you see the world that way and the connections, you see some capacity for action and change in the world by changing those connections. If you say we are connected through the economic market, you can recognize other people so the market is not just, you know, any market; it's not just some abstract economic phenomenon that gets reported on the news at night.

I think we often look at big organizations or the economy as though they're these big things outside of us. I think it's helpful to locate ourselves in the web of connections: we are *doing* economy; we are *doing* politics; we are *doing* community. Community isn't just something that exists out there and you either go into it or you don't. You're part of it. You need to make it better, or worse. The choices we have are about how we are going to participate.

I think sometimes people imagine, when they get into a discussion about these sorts of social and political issues, that they're in the referee's chair and some other people are playing the game and it's just a question of judging those other people: the Republicans are doing this, the Democrats are doing that. What we need is to get out of the referee's chair and recognize that we're in the game, whatever we do, and it's how we participate.

You also asked the question in a way that puts this together with history. The world changes, and that's the reminder that *we* make these connections. I didn't make the global capitalist economy but I do participate in it, and it wasn't just *there*. Even though it's huge, it didn't just happen. It is the result of human action: of selling, industrial production, mass consumption. All these things translate into human action and because of that, human action can change them. There's something liberating in knowing that, as opposed to thinking that they're abstract.

Would you say that you feel hopeful?

Yes, although I would go on to say that I experience being hopeful as who I am and not as a deduction from what I think. There's an old saying on the left of pessimism of the intellect and an optimism of the will. You may analyze all the problems of the world and see all that's there but it's nice if you have the determination to keep seeing solutions. I think it's not just determination. An analysis of the world today sees lots of bad scenarios and lots of problems, so I'm not hopeful because I can see the way out of all those problems; I'm hopeful because that's who I am.

SAM GREEN

In his recent live-scored documentary, *Utopia in Four Movements*, Sam Green probed attempts to realize human dreams (or delusions, depending on the audience). These include a universal language, the world's largest shopping mall, a World's Fair time capsule, and the persistent positivity of an American exile in Cuba.

An enduring concern of Green's is with the tenuous distinction between success and failure. The ending of his Academy Award–nominated documentary *The Weather Underground* encapsulates this tension: Weather member Mark Rudd struggles on camera with his sense of shame over the "things I'm not proud of." Fellow member Naomi Jaffe, on the other hand, resolutely states that she would do it all again.

What compelled you to want to try to contend with the topic of utopia?

I made this movie about the [1960s radical student group] Weather Underground. I wasn't around in the '60s so I had to talk to a lot of people and read a lot of books and I kept coming across this term: "the crisis of leisure time." I was curious; it's such a cool expression. I went to the library—this was the late '90s so you couldn't just Google something—and found a couple of references to it in the '50s and '60s in sociology. There was a legitimate field of study or inquiry related to the crisis of leisure time. What it meant was that with the way automation was going and the standard of living, which was getting so much higher all the time, people thought that, in the future, a big problem was going to be that we'd all have too much leisure time; what are we going to do with it? I had this terrible moment of laughing and crying in the library. The idea of too much leisure time is not even a remote possibility any more.

It made a big impression on me and started me thinking about how different historical moments have different senses of the future and possibility and different kinds of hope, and you live in your own [moment] and you get used to it.

I think if you ask most people today what the future will be like, they would say what I might say: Logically, it's going to be a worse version of the present. There will be more people, less resources, more ecological problems. It's hard to be hopeful. And that, to me, when I thought about it, was a big tragedy because unless you can imagine something better how are you going to get there? It seems like at this very moment our powers of cultural imagination are atrophied. We don't daydream about robots that might do all the work for us the way people did at other points in time. I'm not that interested in utopian communities or a perfect world, but I'm interested in utopia as a gesture; a way of thinking about the future that's radically different and radically better than the present. That, to me, is a beautiful impulse and a valid and healthy and powerful thing to do—to imagine something that is beyond our sense of what's really possible.

What is the most useful definition of utopia?

I say this sincerely: If you look at the early utopians and the early spirit or concept, it's almost always about a collective endeavor or an openness or fairness in terms of resources. It's almost always, in the early articulations of it, a progressive—for lack of a better word—project. If you look at Thomas More, where it sort of came from, that was a critique of inequality at that moment. Sure, there were terrible things in More's utopia, there were slaves, but it came out of an impulse of social critique and a progressive response to inequality. So I do think that that's part of it, even though there is something self-serving about that because it allows me to claim the utopias I like and fence off the ones that I don't. But I think that what utopia has become is a sensibility or project where you radically rewrite the present. There's a kind of a modernist—which I'm really interested in—expression of the utopian impulse where it's like, we're going to tear down Paris and build a whole new city. That is, in some sense, the form of utopia we wrestle with now or the form of it whose shadow we live in.

In the Weather Underground there is a split between past participants who have come to feel that what they did was futile, and those who feel that what they did is still relevant and they're still doing it, just in different ways. How did your opinion of the group and their activities change over the course of making the film?

I was interested in what they did to begin with because I could see both sides. I could see a critique of it. It was loony in a lot of ways, but at the same time I could see the frustration and the sense of urgency that led them to do what they did. Over time it got a little more nuanced, I would talk to somebody who was really against it and it would go back and forth a little bit but at the end of it, maybe I knew more, but I ended up back in the same place where I started. What actually changed me a lot was: I was really nervous meeting all these people because I thought they would be really judgmental of me, you know, "What are you doing for the revolution?" and all that, but they were all really nice people and I became friends with them.

A year or two after I made that film, I was with somebody at a party in the middle of the terrible Bush years. You know when you're at a party how you have stupid conversations and somebody was saying, "Oh, the world sucks," and I found myself saying something I'd never said before. I said, "You just have to have hope irrationally. It's the only way to do it." And I surprised myself, because I realized that I had got that from these people, or it had rubbed off on me. When they were twenty, twenty-five, and were about to "make the revolution," they had all their eggs in one basket and saw the world in such a black and white manner. Twenty-five or thirty years later it didn't happen and they no longer know how to make the revolution or what to do, but they're engaged. And they're engaged without having the big answer. I realized that that was a kind of complex hope. It sort of infected me. I had never had that ability before. Maybe it came from getting a little older, but I saw it as from being exposed to them. It's a really difficult mental jujitsu move to do to yourself and I was very happy that I found myself saying that, because I believe that. I believe that if you can't figure out a way to make hope for yourself then why do anything? Ultimately, being able to be in touch with reality but not necessarily contained by it is the healthiest and most powerful way to think about the world in the future, I think.

Is being an activist different from being radical?

I have a lot of respect for the Weather people and I have a lot of respect for activists in general because most activism is drudge organizing work. I've always felt a little tension between art and activism and I definitely feel like I am an artist as opposed to an activist. It's not my strong point, organizing people. So I respect it. But being radical is different. It seems like there are a lot of ways in which one can be radical. You can be culturally radical, but activism is something else.

What is the tension you feel between art and activism?

For me at least, I feel like the basic impulses are different. The impulse in activism in some way is to make things clear to other people. If you're involved in Occupy Wall Street, you want people to become sensitive to the 1 percent, 99 percent [distinction]. You work to communicate based on clarity and convincing people to see certain things. And art, at least the art I like, is to raise questions and muddy the waters and focus on nuance and all of the complex aspects of human experience that are, to me, most interesting but also most rich. I didn't see the Weather Underground as an activist film even though it resonated with a left audience. I wasn't telling people what to think at all. I make movies that I would want to see and I don't want to be told.

Why is it important to continually approach big questions, even if the intention is not to answer them definitively?

I think to me there's a big difference between asking, "How are we going to make a revolution?" and then you get four baby boomer dudes saying, "It's the workers!" or "It's the students!" I love Occupy but I went to this panel with three different people fighting about whether to have an alternate currency or not. One of the things I really took from the Weather Underground research is that people spent zillions of hours fighting over the answer as to what the proper way was to make revolution and it turned out that they were all wrong. The only lesson I take from that is radical humility. We have no idea, nobody's able to predict how history changes, and rather than throw up your hands, all you can do is do what you're doing but also let everybody do what they're doing. So I have no interest in the question of how we're going to make a revolution but I am fascinated with the question of what revolution might be; how it might work; what is it; will it be a good thing or a bad thing—more the questions around the big questions.

In 2008 I thought for sure that would be a moment, if there were ever going to be a moment, for a radical critique of capitalism. But something weird happened and the moment passed and we're still . . . You know those Socialist Worker's Party members who sell papers and have done for thirty years? I really thought that this was their moment and they'd have people buying their papers but it didn't happen. When I see revolution, in a way I see utopia. There's utopia in the classic sense that I'm not so interested in, but as an impulse . . . And revolution is the same way. I personally would never want to have a violent revolution in this country. I think almost all revolutions are terrible for many people and it's not something to go into lightly at all, but the revolutionary impulse is a great thing and I think it can be channeled in lots of different ways as a wonderful, creative, destructive, inspiring force and we need more of that. So there's a little bit of a distinction, for me at least, between the two. But I think what you're saying—a constellation of ideas, revolution, utopia, creativity, hope—those are all my favorite things.

You have said, regarding the Weather Underground, that they weren't imaginative enough. Can you explain what you meant?

I don't remember saying that but I probably would have said that the Weather Underground was not imaginative enough because they didn't actually have any clear vision for a future. I don't criticize them for that because, in reality, what they were was just a profound "No" to what was happening. At that moment, 2000 people were being killed in Vietnam every single day. If you think about all the horrors of Iraq and Afghanistan, it's nothing compared to that. In 1969 they'd been protesting for five years and things were only getting worse. And it's hard for us to remember but this was not long after the Holocaust, and the big lesson of that had been that you can't just sit by and let things happen in your name. The Weather Underground people had this thing where they said, "We're not going to be good Germans." It was a big epiphany for me to realize that was how they were thinking.

Everybody says, "If I was in the 1800s I'd be friends with the Indians; if I was down South I'd work on the Underground Railroad; if I was near Hitler in the 1930s I'd kill him myself." You can say that because you are never in that situation. [The Weather Underground] felt like they were in that situation. So more than being an imaginative movement about the future, I see them as a radical "No." They never did think [it] through other than socialism, a future, and they weren't even inspired by that. They were driven by the horror of what was happening rather than a hope for what could be—maybe the hope that it could stop, but I think that is one reason why they didn't resonate with a wider public and maybe why, when the Vietnam War ended, they fell apart. They didn't have anything to sustain them but their sense of "No." To me, imagination is really important because it's fun, it's creative, it's positive, it's healthy, it feels good. Creativity and hope are positive things you can do. They didn't have a lot of that. They were dour and driven to this sort of ascetic craziness where they had to stop what was happening. You can't keep that going for very long. You need hope and you need beauty and you need a vision for things being better.

I feel as though imagination has diminished in its value over time.

I think it's diminished in its value and I think we've somehow lost some powers of imagination. And I'm not sure exactly why. It's a really complicated question. Russell Jacoby wrote that it's striking that nobody really writes about this [question] or considers it, but it's true. My own half-baked theory has something to do with hyper-capitalism and a super image-based society. If you start getting into porn, you no longer masturbate with fantasies in your head. In some ways, the present is sort of like porn. The moments to imagine are being squeezed out. Somehow life is so much faster and we're always online. Finding those moments to have quintessential daydreaming experiences are harder and harder but there's something very valuable in that. I also see this as why we don't have imaginations for the future on a cultural level. We don't have fancies about how great things are going to be. You no longer have to imagine anything. That muscle that's hard to use and that takes work is now replaced by, "I've got it already."

ARTHUR BLAUSTEIN

Arthur Blaustein is not a naïve man. Having served on the board of the National Endowment for the Humanities under Bill Clinton, and as chair of the President's National Advisory Council on Economic Opportunity under Jimmy Carter, he has both an innate sense of economic and social policy and a nuanced personal politics.

Perhaps despite his clarity, Blaustein genuinely believes in making a difference and has written numerous books on how volunteering and community action can improve democracy. He is currently a professor of community development, public policy, and politics at the University of California, Berkeley.

❦

When did it become important for you to be politically active?

When I was at graduate school in the '60s, the civil rights movement and then the antiwar movement. It gave me a sense of social justice, the fact that we could actually have an impact on American policy.

What was it about that time that made people mobilize in the way that they did?

The mobilization of the Civil Rights movement came after—I guess it was 1962—people watching the evening news about what was going on in Alabama. Dr. King and the African American community were marching for employment, and the police chief of Birmingham turned on fire hoses and brought out dogs to break up the demonstrations. It was horrid that a civilized society would do that kind of thing. The antiwar sentiment was the draft for most young people. They didn't want to serve in a war they didn't believe in.

In many respects that was a real high point in terms of challenging the status quo and the establishment in a way that has not happened since then. You know, there was the end of apartheid in Africa but that period from 1960 until about 1972 was an anomaly in history.

Is it able to be repeated?

I think it's very possible. I happen to believe—and have taught my students—that, in America, if you look back in history, the 1930s after the Great Depression was the struggle for social justice and that's when we got things like social security, unemployment, child labor laws, a whole variety of things which were part of the social contract that helped to create a middle class, ultimately. The 1960s was the struggle for political justice, and it started with people of color and then went to the women's movement, then to the consumer movement and to the gay movement, which were all outgrowths of the civil rights movement.

My sense is that with Occupy Wall Street, it's been simmering below the surface: the issue of economic injustice. I think there are some real opportunities to mobilize a substantial amount of the citizenry around the issues of economic injustice. However, this issue is more problematic in that most Americans are not educated in school about how economic policy works. What's been brewing is that people feel inadequate to confront the issues or speak out about it because they really don't understand how economic policy is made, but they know to some extent they're being screwed.

What do you think the possibility of economic justice is?

That is a really tough order, primarily because 98 percent of the American public do not understand how American policy is made. We have a terrible educational system when it comes to teaching economics and economic policy. It's not taught on the public school level, it's just charts and graphs that people memorize. Most college economics courses are abstract and theoretical. At most institutions of higher learning, each department is in splendid isolation. Economists are not interested in social consequences or social welfare and the political scientists are not that interested in economic policy or social policy, and that's what's lacking: an understanding that economic justice is quite different from economics. In order to understand public policy and economic policy, you have to understand the comprehensive and coherent relationship between politics, economics, and social policy.

It's interesting to me that you have dealt with these issues while working under presidents Carter and Clinton. You worked within, rather than against, the system you're seeking to affect.

I feel that I accomplished a lot by being inside during the Carter Administration. I was able to save and help continue the institutional base for the anti-poverty programs that really allowed people in low-income communities to survive. We fought every minute to change things. When I was chairman of the Presidents' Council under Carter and, a year later, when Reagan was elected and started to kill programs, we stayed until midnight of the day he put us out of existence. We fought him tooth and nail.

How would you characterize the average American's experience of community?

It's been downhill since the '50s, with the advent of television and then the revolution with computers. More and more people are isolated and what they have is virtual communities rather than real communities. People know more about golf through their golfing community online than they do about health insurance or the zoning in the communities where they live. So the sense of isolation undermines community, undermines values, undermines democracy.

People now know more and more about less and less, and what's lacking is a substantive sense of what democracy means, of what community means, of what justice means, of what freedom means, of what opportunity means—all those issues that are fundamental to a healthy, dynamic society.

So the connection is between community and a certain type of knowledge?

It was T. S. Eliot who once said: information is not knowledge; knowledge is not intelligence; intelligence is not wisdom. And we have a lot of information but very little wisdom.

Emotional connection also seems to play a part in people's relationship to their community, and therefore the extent of their knowledge.

People have an emotional and psychological association to issues. If the news says there are eleven million unemployed, that doesn't give people insight into what happens in a town when the factory packs up and relocates to a third world country. When you're watching television and it's nine million, eleven million unemployed, it's no different from watching a baseball game: Chicago, 9; New York, 11. It doesn't mean anything. You don't know what's happening in the lives of those communities, those families and those workers whose whole identity is tied up in their work. People don't have to deal with it so there's no emotional connection, and that's where good literature comes in, because that's part of moral education. It's fundamental. If you don't have healthy values and decent moral and ethical standards, all the learning isn't going to do any good. This country does not need more lawyers and accountants; it needs more aware, intelligent, discriminating citizens.

What does "awareness" mean?

It means consciousness of what's happening around you and how you relate to that.

How aware do you think society is at present?

On a conscious level, not very. But on a subconscious level, it's there. That's why people responded to Occupy Wall Street. I think that Occupy touched a nerve on a subconscious level of people's anxiety and frustration. The game is being run on people but they don't know how the game is being run.

I've said before that Occupy has done an outstanding service to the American people for bringing up the mal-distribution of wealth and economic justice, but I think the next step, how they're really going to have an impact, is economic education. Occupying space doesn't do very much. If I were advising them I would, in every community where there's a university or a community college, have teach-ins on economic education and how the problems developed and how to solve them. Get people involved; it will give them a sense of community, it will fill a vacuum. It was those kinds of teach-ins that mobilized people against the war in Vietnam. And I see no reason why the next step for Occupy shouldn't be economic teach-ins.

[Occupy] raises the issue of economic justice and mal-distribution of wealth. It's out there. It's being discussed. Thomas Jefferson once wrote, you can be free or ignorant—you can't be both. To the extent you're ignorant of how economic decisions that affect economic justice are made, it's not going to mean anything to occupy physical space. You have to occupy mental space, psychological space, to get people connected with the issues in ways that they understand, that are consistent with healthy values, that are consistent with building a better community, and that can put bread and butter on the table for their families. That next step is economic education.

You said that education gives people the freedom to make choices. I get the sense that this freedom is not just the freedom to make choices but to actually realize that there are options.

Somewhere in the '70s, and it was reinforced with Reagan in the '80s, the goal of this country and of individuals and of success became quantitative rather than qualitative. And we had a shift from qualitative values to quantitative values. The quantitative values—having 118 channels that say nothing—are not freedom. They are sold on the grounds of freedom, like twenty-six flavors of ice cream that are not good for you. That's quantitative rather than qualitative, and qualitative things are those human things that are going to make the difference between having a humane, decent society and not having one.

If you had children, what would be the one thing you would really want them to know?

There would be a lot of things. But I think what I learned when I was young was empathy, whether compassion or empathy or moral intelligence, that kind of sensibility. That's why each of the books that I've done has had a purpose to it. I believe that one of the reasons I wrote [*Democracy Is Not a Spectator Sport*] is because of my experience particularly with young people. They have for the last twenty years not been involved in political action before the Obama campaign. But I have found when you get them to volunteer in the community and they see what's going on in the city or the schools or the health centers, it changes them and they start to make connections and realize that the way to make change is through political action.

You have said before that Occupy Wall Street's trajectory is in history. Can you explain what you mean?

Well, I am a product of the '60s. Martin Luther King talked about the arc of history and this was before President Kennedy and President Johnson decided to implement the Civil Rights Act and the Voting Rights Act. King, in his heart and soul, knew that he was on the side of the arc of history. In order to be able to teach, in order to be able to write, I have to believe I am on the side of justice and peace and that justice and peace are on the side of history. You have to believe it—otherwise you don't go out every day and do it.

Let me tell you a story: A friend of mine in Maine was a volunteer for a nonprofit organization. Either Senator Edward or Robert Kennedy's son started a fuel co-op because the big issues in Maine were heating, oil and gas, and they organized co-ops and got people to participate. One day, this friend of mine who was an organizer and had set up about thirty co-ops was giving a talk in a town hall with a group of farmers and townspeople. All of a sudden a guy from Portland, from the evening news, was standing outside in the hallway. Before the vote of whether to join the co-op, people came out into the hallway and this TV anchor newsman was there, and he said to a farmer, "What do you think about all this outside agitation?"

That farmer, on camera, had a face that looked just like Percy Kilbride, the actor who played a New England farmer and did the commercials for Pepperidge Farm cookies. The farmer looked into the camera and said, "There are two kinds of politics and economics in America: the first kind is what politicians tell me when they want my vote and what I see on the evening news; the second kind is what me and my friends talk about over donuts and coffee, and that's what that young fellow was talking about tonight and I'm joining the co-op." And that's the same thing as Occupy, the nerve it struck. It was what they were talking about over donuts and coffee. That's the kind of economics and politics that people want to engage with in this country, and that need to be elevated.

SEYLA BENHABIB

Seyla Benhabib is the Eugene Mayer Professor of Political Science and Philosophy at Yale University, and directed Ethics, Politics, and Economics from 2002 to 2008. As a democratic theorist she argues that the formation of cultures is likewise contingent on dialogue with other cultures and that competing narratives of individual and collective identity are inherent in a healthy society.

Her published works include *Politics in Dark Times: Encounters with Hannah Arendt* and *The Rights of Others: Aliens, Citizens and Residents*, winner of the Ralph Bunche award from the American Political Science Association.

Describe for me what you would consider to be your first political experience.

I grew up in a Sephardic Jewish family in Istanbul. We were Spanish Jews who came out of the Inquisition in Spain into the Ottoman provinces, Istanbul, and Salonica. I grew up in a family that spoke three languages, Turkish, Spanish, and French and then English, but English was the language of instruction from the time I was eleven. I went to an English High School for Girls for five years from 1961 to 1966, and then to an American college for girls from 1966 to 1970. I would say that I grew up in an environment where one was extremely cultured about being, so-called, a religious and ethnic minority, in a country that was trying to become a democratic republic.

And this was an experiment. My classmates were Greek, Armenian, British, German, etcetera—Istanbul was an extremely cosmopolitan city at the time. But my political awakening started with the Vietnam War. Before that there was political sensibility in terms of being a quote unquote, "religious minority, an ethnic minority," and, you know, hearing about how the government dealt or did not deal with certain kinds of things. But when I was in the American college for girls, the Vietnam War was escalating and some of our teachers were either draft resisters or they were conscientious objectors. They were really opposed to the war and they started circulating leaflets and other information about what America was doing in Vietnam at that time. I would say that that experience—seeing napalm bombs having scarred the skin of Vietnamese children—that was an incredible, incredible moment!

Along with that, there were developments in Turkish society where for the first time there was an independent workers' movement, and this workers' movement was predominantly socialist. When I was a senior in 1969, about to graduate from the American college for girls, there was an incredible confrontation between what was then called the Revolutionary Workers' Syndicate Council (DISK) and the Turkish government's military forces. The bridge that joined two sides of Istanbul—the Asian and the European side—was drawn apart. This meant that you could not get from one side of the city to another.

This all happened within a span of three years—'66 to '69. The Vietnam War, on the one hand, and developments at home on the other. I would say that I had political sensibility before that, but these were really experiences that were political experiences.

Perhaps it is because of this personal engagement from early on that, in your capacity as political philosopher, you conduct yourself with a social responsibility that extends beyond an academic context.

If we try to think not just about promoting an academic career—and here I'm deeply indebted to Hannah Arendt—if we try to think about "what we're doing," what we're doing always involves some kind of existential commitment, some kind of burning early commitment, something from your gut and in your heart and in your veins that makes you move. I mean, there are brilliant philosophers and thinkers for whom you also have the feeling that it's just in the brain. Wittgenstein is someone I deeply admire, but Wittgenstein was all in the brain. I know enough about his autobiography to know that there's also an existential moment in his turn to philosophy, but he sublimates it. For him it becomes this question about speech and language games. For me, it's not that way. It's much more on the surface: I'm trying to think something through from the very beginning, which is what it means to be a citizen—a political subject of a modern, modernizing entity—and what it means to be the "other" in whatever ways in which you can identify that otherness.

What does a political subject constitute?

I would say that today, in the first decade of the twenty-first century, we are facing the disappearance of the political subject. I am not sure. My generation experienced politics when we were seventeen, eighteen years old in various ways. One of my earliest political memories is a friend inviting me to go to an anti-NATO demonstration in the 1960s. At the time I was in Istanbul and I said, "No, I can't go because I have home-work to do this afternoon, let's talk later." My friend went, and he needed stitches in his head when he returned because the Turkish police had at-tacked the demonstrators.

I became an adult with that kind of political experience, and then lived through the repression of the Kurdish language rights, even at that point. The political world was present to us in a very palpable way. At some points you sort of took sides for life. Whose side are you on? This was not an academic question, it was right there. If you have your friends beaten up, you go down to the streets and you see people being shot . . .

What does it mean to be a political subject? Something has really changed. Part of it is that we are living in this age of huge mass de-mocracies that are televisually connected. The political parties themselves in almost every country of the world have changed. Left and right no longer mean a thing. The terms came from the seating of the parties in the French Revolutionary Assembly after 1789, but what does that mean today? I'm not saying that there are no differences, there are, but the dif-ferences have become increasingly less salient. They still make a difference in elections, but they don't really make the kind of difference that they did I think for much of the nineteenth and certainly the twentieth century.

Then you have the media. You have the televisual public sphere. This medium is a very strange medium because sometimes images say more and subliminally suggest more, and they create more connections than deliberation and argumentative speech. I think what you are seeing in general is a trend toward less deliberative politics. Politics is less about de-liberation and resolution, and it is more about emotional and subliminal identification, replete with images and posturing.

Together with the collapse of the party system and televisual political culture, what emerges is a new kind of political subjectivity that is quite confused, easily malleable, and it's hard to know what it means to be a political subject under these conditions when so much of traditional po-litical institutions no longer seem to prevail.

I was listening to an Egyptian colleague today at a meeting and he was talking about the significance of the virtual social media. For him the social media is real as a source of power. We know what a role it played in the Arab Revolution, in the Arab Spring. It certainly is extremely important but it's certainly not enough. You can get people out on to the streets but you can't get them to the next stage to know how to build a government or to manage the rules of parliamentary discussion. I think that the Egyptian people have done remarkably well despite all the shenanigans and so on that are going on with the military, the young people have been very, very clear and clever strategic subjects. But if you become a political subject in this virtual space, then what are the institutions? How do you still build that? It's a changing landscape.

I would argue that recent events seem to suggest a re-politicization of public life in America. Is what you're saying not necessarily quantitative, just an acknowledgement of change?

I would like to hope so, not just hope in a vague sense. I mean, for me, the principle of hope is also a principle of acting for the future, and acting to change the future, to be an agent of the future. I certainly felt very proud of Occupy Wall Street. [Before Occupy] you said to yourself, how long are people in the United States going to take it? How long is this going to go on?

And it's interesting too that it was not [only] people who are devastated by the mortgage crisis who are losing their homes, their schools— it's not those people—but primarily young individuals who are educated and see themselves facing a world of debt, but who have expectations, who have articulation, who went out onto the streets. It's always like this. Revolutions or reform movements, opposition, always happen in periods of rising expectations as well as frustrations.

[To be] a political subject, it is never, never impossible, I don't think so. Even totalitarianism runs itself out after a certain time and the space for politics presents itself. There are always ways to act differently and to have imagination and power.

It's interesting that you say "imagination." As much as any social movement has to be practical, I feel as though it's equally realistic to say that there must also be an imaginative element.

Absolutely. I think that one tends to confuse imagination with fantasy or fiction. And there's nothing wrong with fantasy or fiction, but imagination is a very complex faculty. I could talk about the significance of imagination in my political philosophy and so on, but I'm not going to do that. What I'm going to say is that what one needs to think about is "reconfiguration." An imaginative individual does not simply propagate things, but either reconfigures or rearticulates, reshapes in such a way that you can see the "new" in it. The "new" bears some relationship to the "real," in quotation marks, if I may put it that way.

So imagination is a reconfiguring of the elements. And what really impressed me about the Occupy Wall Street movement, although there was no theory about it in that way, is that all of a sudden they took over this strange space, Zuccotti Park. It isn't just a space that is within the earshot of Wall Street, it's also, if you walk three blocks, [near] the 9/11 Memorial. It's a space where the old and the new come together. It's a kind of space that is home to strange and unexplored historical significations for this country, for the United States. I mean, the disaster of the Twin Towers, and the construction site, is right next to the park.

I went down there twice, and on one morning I went down there [I noticed] that you had to walk through this gaping Wall Street construction before you could get to Zuccotti Park, which is a small city space in the middle of all these dark, cavernous buildings. It was a space that the private realtor had made public, and there's also that strange category of the private that is made public. It's not somebody's backyard, and it's not exactly Central Park.

So it took imagination, if I may put it this way, to resignify that space as a public space for the Occupation. I don't know who came up with this idea, but I'd like to congratulate them. It was really an active imagination, because [Zuccotti Park's] proximity to the two symbolic centers—it had to be within earshot of Wall Street, [who] make people feel bad—and then also the Twin Towers—is really very complex. There is that dual imaginative act going on. People haven't really talked about this second dimension. I mean why that space? Wall Street is obvious, but why the second relationship to the Twin Towers that has not been explored.

Why do you think?

I don't think this choice was conscious. I think it was subliminal. For a lot of people the reality of American decline, the reality of American malaise and ill-being started with the events of 9/11. That's the point at which the Giant got wounded—and that wound is still there, because there's a gaping space that has not been reconstructed ten years later, eleven years later, you still see it. I haven't read anything from the Occupy Wall Street movement talking about this connection, but maybe subliminally they were also going to that space where they felt that something really tremendous and monumental had happened that affected their generation.

I do think that the movement has benefitted from the lack of too much direct analysis.

It just seems to be a period where we are post–"grand theories." I believe that a lot [of Occupy] was talking intuitively and subliminally at the level at which something is not right for people in their guts, but they did not have the language to express it. I really would love to hear more of the discussion, the full aspects of the symbolic space that they occupied. Every space has its own imaginative topography, right? And so to go back to the theme of the imagination—the imagination is important in selecting the site of your political action, and it's also important in articulating what you do. There was a branch of the movement later on when people were going to build old bridges, bridges that were nearly falling apart and that is such a good metaphor for the complete failure of public investment. That is again an act of imagination. Politics is always about reconfiguring, resignifying the completely familiar into the strange and the unfamiliar. It makes you think, okay, why are people walking towards this defunct bridge? What if they fall into the river? Well, that's precisely the point. What is the government going to do about it?

It is always of interest to me to ask people what defines a time of crisis. We are used to "crisis" seeming so distant, or as belonging to other parts of the world, but Occupy seemed to acknowledge that America had reached a point of crisis just in its own particular way.

I have thought about this conflict of crisis for a long time because it is a crucial concept in left thought, and particularly Marxist left thought. What is the relationship between critique and crisis? I don't want to get scholastic on you, but this was my first book, *Critique, Norm, and Utopia* in 1986. "Crisis" comes from the Greek, as so many other concepts do, and crisis is a moment in the evolution or the progress of a disease when the doctor has to make a judgment. We still say, "The patient is in critical condition," so it's [about] critical judgment. There's always this notion of a juncture, of a turning point associated with the term "crisis." And that's why the term crisis is so important for revolutionary theory, for radical theory. It always signifies a turning point.

I like to think that we have to hold on to that term, but we can no longer have the kind of genealogy associated with it. It seems to me that modernity is lurching from one crisis to another. The capitalist economy, a lot of economists will tell you, goes through cycles of fifty-year crises. Capitalism is a crisis within an economic system. But there's also crises of modernity, because modernity is a process of continuously inventing oneself, reimagining oneself, reconfiguring oneself individually and collectively. There perpetuates a kind of instability that is at the heart of the modern project, and that is at once liberating, and scary.

And you say are we undergoing a kind of general crisis in the United States? Yes, but something feels qualitatively different this time, although again one cannot exaggerate what feels qualitatively different. The language of politics is changing.

One way to think about it, perhaps, is that crisis opens the possibility for something both better and worse than the current situation. But surely people would not act unless they believed in the positive potential.

I think this is absolutely right. Every generation rediscovers the public world for itself and envisages its possible future, absolutely. What we can do, we members of a different generation than yours, is communicate the vocabulary and the experience and maybe provide you with some categories that have their origins in these previous experiences. The world can always be made anew, and I don't think human life is really worth it if one didn't believe in that. And that's why even though when I went down to Occupy Wall Street early on a Sunday morning, all I saw was a bunch of sleepy kids coming out of their sleeping bags, I said, "This is the revolutionary subject," but dirtier. Why not? What did I look like at that age? You have to ask yourself that and hope that they will set right what we may have messed up.

LISA ROBERTSON AND MATTHEW STADLER

Lisa Robertson is a writer. Her published works evade genre, although some resemble poetic and essayistic styles. These include *The Weather*, *R's Boat*, *The Men: A Lyric Book*, and *Occasional Works and Seven Walks from the Office for Soft Architecture*.

Matthew Stadler is a writer and editor. He is the author of four novels, a reader [*Where We Live Now: An Annotated Reader*] and numerous essays concerning sprawl and urbanism. He is also the co-founder, with Patricia No, of Publication Studio, a print-on-demand service. He has argued that publication is "the creation of a public, it is essentially a political act."

Robertson and Stadler compiled, annotated, and published *Revolution: An Annotated Reader* late last year. The 1,000-plus-page document features an extended bibliography from poet David Brazil and texts from Jean Genet, Jacques Rancière, and J. Krishnamurti, among others. The texts are divided into chapters that emulate the human life span: "Beginning," "Childhood," "Education," "Adulthood," and "Death."

How did you come to put together a reader on revolution?

Matthew Stadler: Lisa was, in addition to her own writing, teaching at an art school in San Francisco, and there are a number of readings about revolution from the English Romantics.

Lisa Robertson: It was a seminar on revolution in relation to romantic literature from the seventeenth to the nineteenth century.

MS: I had recently finished a reader on cities. The reader was annotated and I thought I would like to read the same reader on revolution. But that was a while ago and I didn't have any means of support to help her find time for that work. Last spring I had a project going on with the L'Ecole des Beaux Arts du Bordeaux—that was going to include the production of a book using a Publication Studio setup. With that opportunity I returned to this idea and asked Lisa if she'd be into it.

LR: I'm trying to backtrack and think of the context when I was putting that course together. I mean, why was I interested in talking about revolution to American undergraduates in an art school in 2008? I had already been living in France for quite a few years and had been seeing the popular uprisings happening here. There was one in 2008, I went there and there were shells of cars lining the boulevard. So I'd been living in that context in France, where popular uprising is pretty much par for the course, you know? It's what people do here. There's a tradition of radical resistance to injustice. So I came from the French tradition into the United States and felt like I wanted to infect the art students with a bit of this French attitude but from a historical perspective, so that they could see it historically in creative practice. As a non–United Statesian, I feel when I'm invited to that country to participate in their culture, the most responsible thing I can do is to try to infect the youth.

The historical texts in the reader are almost like education for articulating discontent.

MS: I hope it doesn't only help articulate discontent, I think quite a few of the selections are meant to create a space of contentment.

LR: Pleasure is a large part of revolution. You have no interest in changing the status quo if you don't already have an investment in living as being bountiful and positive, and wild.

MS: [The reader] was so much work there would be no way to do it if you didn't totally love each text. A lot of my feeling as we were going through that work was a feeling of desire, of, "I want to live in this." And that feeling would be hard if we were being more calculated and instrumental about our choices, I think.

LR: I guess we could say that non-instrumentalized step is one step up of a revolutionary stance. It's the instrumentalization of economic life, effective exchange, everything communicational and cultural that revolution has to refuse.

The idea of embodiment comes up several times in the reader.

LR: The criteria that we did have overtly is that each one of the writers of these texts put themselves in a position where they were able to perceive what was already revolutionary in the present, in life, as it was being lived. So that a revolutionary stance doesn't have to do with transforming yourself into somebody else, it doesn't have to do with changing your vocabulary, it doesn't have to do necessarily with changing your daily life. It has to do with recognizing what aspects of dealing with experience of life are already overflowing in any sort of structure.

I think that the criteria of revolution as always already happening in the present has to do with embodiment because, you know, that's where we begin. We begin with how our bodies meet the world; how our bodies are constituted by the world. It's with that very intimate yet nevertheless collective series of recognitions that revolution can begin. And whether you call it the present or whether you call it embodiment is, you know, a similar texture of recognition and commitment to current conditions.

In the introduction you wrote: "What does revolution look like? This book is an attempt to teach ourselves to see and be seen." Can you explain this to me?

LR: "Seeing and being seen" is sort of simplified vocabulary for talking about recognition. In the history of revolutionary discourse, recognition is central to transforming the present into a resistant and positive force. It's a term that Hegel uses in his work. Recognition is central to community formation: How do we recognize one another? How do we stop using one another? How do we stop seeing our relationship as being instrumental, and start experiencing relationships as radical opportunities for collective recognition?

We think of the word "recognition" as perceiving what you recognize in somebody else. But it's also got the word "cognition" inside it, and it has to do with the plenitude of our mental lives as being something that happens between people. And it's that plenitude that is revolutionary. That plenitude that's not originating from a singular point of identity, but is originating from the complexity of various individuals and the intensities that circulate among individuals as recognition.

MS: There's a way in which these issues do overlap with some of the lived experience of Occupy, at least for me. I was only at the Portland one, which was quite massive, but the definitive aspect of it to me was this commitment to physically be there. That was it. It was the fact that our bodies are going to be together here now.

Tell me about your decision to include "Death" as a chapter in the reader, as a stage that is in itself revolutionary.

LR: We wanted to have all the parts of life present and death is part of life. It's a fact, whether you're trying to avoid it or whether you're trying to understand it. Death gets used as a weapon against people. The fear of death is the main way of controlling populations, covertly or overtly. So it seems like the best thing to do is not to let it be a taboo. The American cultural and religious attitude towards death is that it's something that's hidden that doesn't have to do with life, that doesn't have to do with political life. This is what people thought about "women's issues" until a few decades ago, that it didn't really have to do with the important parts of life. We choose to bring childhood into revolution and we chose to bring death into revolution because revolution must include everything.

As you say, a few chapters before "Death," there is a chapter on "Childhood."

MS: That was [to do with] the initial frustration about the ways in which revolution is written. For me, it was positioned as an adolescent phenomenon whether literally or metaphorically. It is written as a rebellion, a rallying up against authority that mimics what we understand in adolescence. I've always been frustrated by that view of adolescence and more so frustrated that the political potential should be pinioned and limited that way. I think Lisa had told me about Louise Michel ["Vroncourt"], and there were a number of texts I had been reading about kids.

The experience of revolution articulated within childhood and within stories of childhood really just blows open, and I think overcomes, any narrow idea about adolescence. Its positioning disappears as soon as you recognize the complexity of children and childhood experience. The idea that you exceed perceived or administered limits is very much [present] in that understanding of childhood—but that was an afterthought.

LR: One thing I don't think we were thinking about at all when we were making our selections or annotating was children and revolution in relation to the English Romantic conception of childhood. Their view on childhood was that it was revolutionary. There were big changes later in Wordsworth's career, but when he began writing *The Prelude*, for example, about his own childhood, it was to look to childhood as a source for non-hegemonic experience. I'm not setting up English Romanticism as some sort of be-all and end-all model for how to conduct one's life and conversations, but I find that interesting.

This is something I think we think about a lot in feminist thought: What happens to little girls when they're socialized into adolescent femininity? They're socialized out of their wildness. And there can be a huge nostalgia about that. What happened to that pre-puberty wildness of little girls who fought viciously and did everything that females are supposedly not interested in? That's always interested me to think about that in relation to gender formation and the centralization of femininity in our culture. Thinking of my own and other people's childhood experiences and relationships and friendships really models how I'd prefer to be living now. You take a few dozen books into your bed and read with a flashlight. You make forts and you run wild. You live outside all summer long. You don't sleep in a house. You know?

MS: And you constantly insist on living. One important recognition is that, when we read our way through these experiences—some of them positioned in children, some of them positioned in very old people, some of them positioned in dying—we recognize that all of it happens at any age. It's not an age-based set of experiences. It's each of these things that can happen across a life.

LAWRENCE FERLINGHETTI

I contacted Lawrence Ferlinghetti once more after we met to ask about the germination of his politics. He told me that, prior to arriving in San Francisco, "I was totally straight and totally naive in politics, the all-American boy scout, thank you. I became politically educated by listening to KPFA/FM and was especially influenced by the presence and radical writings of Kenneth Rexroth."

Ferlinghetti is a poet, artist, and co-founder of City Lights booksellers and publishers. He is former poet laureate of San Francisco and a Commandeur de l'Ordre des Arts et des Lettres. Like Rexroth, he has come to influence successive generations in both politics and poetics.

In *Poetry As Insurgent Art*, he writes, "If you would be a poet, create works capable of answering the challenge of apocalyptic times, even if this meaning sounds apocalyptic."

***

How do you see America at present?

It's a totally different world now in the twenty-first century than in the twentieth century. Not just America. The whole ballgame has changed. The old culture is going down the drain faster than anyone realizes, just disappearing practically overnight. The dumbing down of America through television, in government policies, about education, means a population that's semi-literate and brainwashed.

If I had asked you the same question maybe in the late 1950s, what would you have said?

Oh well, that's a different world completely. I didn't know anyone who had television here in the '50s. Where are you based?

New York.

I've heard of that place, is that the little island? Yeah, I was born there. In the 1950s, when I arrived in San Francisco, it was still the last frontier and it was still a small provincial capital. Everything was still possible here. During World War II, a lot of the population got recruited and went to war and then, when the war was over, a lot of the population came home briefly but then took off for the West [Coast]. They call that "The Greatest Generation," as if the whole continent tilted westward and the population slid to the West Coast. It took almost a decade for the emerging culture to coalesce into a new radical American culture, which was totally different than before World War II.

And it happened in San Francisco. It didn't happen in New York, it didn't happen in Paris. Paris '68 came later, inspired by what had started in San Francisco. The poetry movement that started here couldn't have happened in New York. The New York poets came out here because things were wide open, and they weren't getting any place in New York, like Ginsberg in school. This is where it all began, the '60s and the counterculture. By the time the Beatles came along and the student revolutions happened, it was sweeping around the world. All the aspects of counterculture were absorbed into the general middle class, so you had tie-dyed shirts sold in the suburbs of Bronxville, New York. Today you look around and you'd think the '60s never happened, but actually it was so integrated into the general culture that it's not noticeable any more.

The cultural revolution happened in the '60s but the political revolution, meaning the taking over of the government, never happened. [The '60s] had lots of separate revolutions like women's lib and gay lib and you got all these mini-revolutions but it's no political takeover of the government. So the same imperialist capitalist corporate status is still ruling everything.

Do you think people will always seek improvement of their society?

Not necessarily. Everyone is out for themselves. That's why capitalism has spread around the world. It's a system for allowing everyone to get whatever they can without any social consequence. Although, you know, I was on Amy Goodman's *Democracy Now* program and I asked her, "Do you think the day will ever arrive where conditions will be such that you will no longer have to dissent?" And I don't believe she gave me any answer. In the history of the last hundred years, there's always been too much to dissent about. I don't think there'll ever be a day when there's nothing to dissent about. Then you'd just have paradise on earth or something, but even if you had paradise on earth, Tarzan would still want two Janes [laughs]. And another Tarzan on the other side of the country, he'll want two Janes also, so it's a hopeless situation.

Is making art always a political act?

No, it's not always political. Well, from another point of view, it is—because you can say that even the most non-political art makes a political statement just by opting out of the political system; in other words, by writing a poem about a star, the fact that you chose to write a poem about a star instead of about suffering people somewhere, by your choice, you've made a political statement. Bertolt Brecht had a poem a long time ago: "What times are these, in which a conversation about trees is almost a crime, for in doing so we maintain our silence about so much wrongdoing." A poem about love is almost a sin because it contains so many silences about so many atrocities.

What do art and poetry offer that other forms of dissent do not?

Well, you have what's called a "lyric escape." You can say that the world is coming to an end, that there's a steamroller approaching and we're all going to be flattened but if you decide to turn your back and read a beautiful poem by Keats, for instance: "a thing of beauty is a joy forever, it will never fade into nothingness," that's what I call a "lyric escape," which is a form of dissent 'cause you've decided not to join the dominant society or the dominant culture.

When I use the term "dominant culture," it recalls the fact that—going back for a moment to the '60s revolution—Herbert Marcuse, who was a Marxist philosopher, noted the great capacity of capitalist society or the dominant culture to ingest its own most dissident elements. And this is what happened in the '60s. So many of the people and groups in the '60s considered themselves revolutionary: everyone from rock bands to poets to country-western singers. Then the ones who made it big, like quite a few of the rock groups and the various writers, well, we used to say they "sold out," but they were ingested by the system. They became too well-fed and then they didn't protest anymore.

I mean, look at what happened to Hemingway, although Hemingway was from an earlier generation. His book on the Spanish Civil War, *For Whom the Bell Tolls*, was really from a leftist position. Later on he was living in Cuba and I was on the American Fair Play for Cuba Committee and we wrote him and tried to get him to write a letter supporting our committee and supporting the Cuban Revolution, but we never even heard from him. From our point of view, he was completely sold out and wasn't the man he used to be.

You could say that none of the Beat poets, like Allen Ginsberg, were ever ingested by the system. Even though he made a lot of money—not by today's standards I mean, the annual royalties that he used to get from City Lights Books, when I was his principal editor, were never more than maybe $15,000 a year. But at that time, it was quite a bit of money and it was a lot of money for a poet to make and yet by the end of every year, he was completely broke because he was supporting so many people and giving his money away. By the time it was time to pay him his next royalty check, he was totally without a cent and that happened right up to the end. Even when he was dying, he was calling people up, friends of his around the country to say, "Do you need anything? Do you need some money?" So, he was a good example of someone who didn't get ingested.

Why do you think the ideas of you and your contemporaries, which were quite outside of social norms at that time, resonated with people?

Well, we were talking the talk; I hope we still are. When I first read *Howl*, when I first heard Ginsberg read it, I said, "I've never seen the world in that light before." There was a whole new world and a whole new way of seeing everything and a new sensibility, a new consciousness of the time, which Ginsberg and Gregory Corso and William Burroughs and Jack Kerouac and Gary Snyder were articulating.

Do you think that ideas that used to concern many people fifty or sixty years ago now concern few?

I feel as though fifty years ago it was quite common for someone's politics and their sense of pop culture to sort of fit together; and now, they seem quite distinct and it's almost as though you have to make a choice to be political, it doesn't just come to people naturally.

So, what do you think it would take for people to become interested in the way that they once were?

I don't know. The whole country is certainly brainwashed by television and you notice that even the adult programs on television and the ads that go with the adult television, there are all these little widgets and gimmicks and imaginary figures. It's like all of television is aimed at someone about eight years old. Then if you get to a big sports event like the Super Bowl, the halftime show is very, very militaristic. They have a band dressed up as soldiers with guns and, always, of course, they have to sing The National Anthem. It's pure, rampant nationalism.

What could change it? What could speak to people that hasn't yet?

It would take a revolution, of course, but what kind of revolution? Wouldn't it be a surprise to the United States and the other capitalist countries if some of these revolutions in the Arab countries, these revolutionary movements, chose socialism instead of capitalism?

I mean, there's a big battle going on in Egypt right now for control of the movement and it's quite likely that it'll go in some socialist direction rather than capitalism. The trouble with the Occupy Wall Street movement is that—quite rightly—they didn't choose any one political ideology because as soon as they choose one political ideology, whether it be socialism or anarchism or whatever, then about half the people would drop out because they'd say, "Well, I don't agree with that ideology." So they had a great advantage in not choosing an ideology but then it comes to the point where sooner or later they're going to have to articulate an ideology. It just might not be any of the old ideologies because it could work out that a new ideology is what would be needed.

What potential do you see for that to happen?

Well, I don't know where it's going to come from. The reason the political revolution of the '60s never happened was because all anyone could think of was imported foreign ideologies. There were Maoist groups and communist groups and socialist groups but there was no American ideology, and that's the trouble today.

I think the ecological catastrophe that's descending on us is liable to be the factor of change because while Congress is debating how many millionaires can dance on the head of a pin, the ecological situation is getting worse and worse every minute and it's never mentioned. I think one day they're going to wake up with this big wave over their head and they'll say, "Oh, I didn't even notice it was creeping up on us!"

The name of my next book is *The Time of Useful Consciousness*. It's an aeronautical term that refers to the time between when you're deprived of oxygen and when you pass out. That short space of time, that's when you still can do something to save yourself.

And you feel like we're in that time now?

Yeah! We are! And it's quite a short time.

Although you must feel some hope otherwise you wouldn't bother to write the book.

Well, not necessarily [laughs]. You keep writing even if there were no hope.

Let me ask you about Poetry As An Insurgent Art. *Who did you write that for?*

I wrote it mostly for poets so that most of 'em would take their head out of the sands and be revolutionary. But *Insurgent Art* is still just a drop in the bucket. If you add up all the print media together they're just one percent of the electronic media, so you can say there's not much hope in changing the world through print.

Do you think that, to an extent, society today is answerable to the '60s?

Yeah, that's the discourse we have to continue. Those are the terms of the discourse; we don't have any other. And the '60s tried to break out of that but then they didn't come up with any ideology that was new.

It seems today that no one gives a damn anymore. It's like, "Get yours!" and then, "To hell with everyone else!" It's such a cynical age now. Actually, I wish Allen Ginsberg were still around. He was always a very enlightened being; he was always probing and wondering, "Well, what's the best way to do this or that?" I remember when we were on stage at the

Human Be-In, which was in Golden Gate Park in 1968, or was it '67? And we're on stage there with—good God—Timothy Leary [laughs], Gary Snyder, and Michael McClure. You know, there were 10,000 people out there in this great meadow and a parachutist comes down, parachutes into the crowd, just when the sun was setting and everyone goes, "Ah-hhhh!" Ten thousand people going "Ahhhhh!" Everyone on the stage is doing their thing and I'm sitting next to Allen and he turns and whispers to me, "What if we're all wrong?" That's the way he was; he wasn't a dogmatic leader who would tell what you should be doing except something like, "Don't smoke! Don't smoke! Don't smoke! Don't smoke!" [laughs].

How do we answer that question, "What if we're all wrong?"

Well, you have to question everything. Question absolutely everything.